Understanding
American History

Prohibition

Stephen Currie

Bruno Leone
Series Consultant

ReferencePoint
Press®

San Diego, CA

© 2013 ReferencePoint Press, Inc.
Printed in the United States

For more information, contact:
ReferencePoint Press, Inc.
PO Box 27779
San Diego, CA 92198
www. ReferencePointPress.com

LIBRARY OF CONGRESS CATALOGING-IN-PUBLICATION DATA

Currie, Stephen, 1960-
  Prohibition / by Stephen Currie.
     p. cm. -- (Understanding american history)
  Includes bibliographical references and index.
  ISBN-13: 978-1-60152-508-6 (hbk. : alk. paper)
  ISBN-10: 1-60152-508-7 (hbk. : alk. paper)
  1. Prohibition--United States--Juvenile literature. 2. United States--History--20th century--Juvenile literature. I. Title.
  HV5089.C84 2013
  363.4'10973--dc23
                                                                    2012038100

Contents

Foreword

America's Puritan ancestors—convinced that their adopted country was blessed by God and would eventually rise to worldwide prominence—proclaimed their new homeland the shining "city upon a hill." The nation that developed since those first hopeful words were uttered has clearly achieved prominence on the world stage and it has had many shining moments but its history is not without flaws. The history of the United States is a virtual patchwork of achievements and blemishes. For example, America was originally founded as a New World haven from the tyranny and persecution prevalent in many parts of the Old World. Yet the colonial and federal governments in America took little or no action against the use of slave labor by the southern states until the 1860s, when a civil war was fought to eliminate slavery and preserve the federal union.

In the decades before and after the Civil War, the United States underwent a period of massive territorial expansion; through a combination of purchase, annexation, and war, its east–west borders stretched from the Atlantic to the Pacific Oceans. During this time, the Industrial Revolution that began in eighteenth-century Europe found its way to America, where it was responsible for considerable growth of the national economy. The United States was now proudly able to take its place in the Western Hemisphere's community of nations as a worthy economic and technological partner. Yet America also chose to join the major western European powers in a race to acquire colonial empires in Africa, Asia, and the islands of the Caribbean and South Pacific. In this scramble for empire, foreign territories were often peacefully annexed but military force was readily used when needed, as in the Philippines during the Spanish-American War of 1898.

Toward the end of the nineteenth century and concurrent with America's ambitions to acquire colonies, its vast frontier and expanding industrial base provided both land and jobs for a new and ever-growing wave of immigrants from southern and eastern Europe. Although America had always encouraged immigration, these newcomers—Italians, Greeks, and eastern European Jews, among others—were seen as different from the vast majority of earlier immigrants, most of whom were from northern and western Europe. The presence of these newcomers was treated as a matter of growing concern, which in time evolved into intense opposition. Congress boldly and with calculated prejudice set out to create a barrier to curtail the influx of unwanted nationalities and ethnic groups to America's shores. The outcome was the National Origins Act, passed in 1924. That law severely reduced immigration to the United States from southern and eastern Europe. Ironically, while this was happening, the Statue of Liberty stood in New York Harbor as a visible and symbolic beacon lighting the way for people of *all* nationalities and ethnicities seeking sanctuary in America.

Unquestionably, the history of the United States has not always mirrored that radiant beacon touted by the early settlers. As often happens, reality and dreams tend to move in divergent directions. However, the story of America also reveals a people who have frequently extended a helping hand to a weary world and who have displayed a ready willingness—supported by a flexible federal constitution—to take deliberate and effective steps to correct injustices, past and present. America's private and public philanthropy directed toward other countries during times of natural disasters (such as the contributions of financial and human resources to assist Haiti following the January 2010 earthquake) and the legal right to adopt amendments to the US Constitution (including the Thirteenth Amendment freeing the slaves and the Nineteenth Amendment granting women the right to vote) are examples of the nation's generosity and willingness to acknowledge and reverse wrongs.

With objectivity and candor, the titles selected for the Understanding American History series portray the many sides of America, depicting both its shining moments and its darker hours. The series strives to help readers achieve a wider understanding and appreciation of the American experience and to encourage further investigation into America's evolving character and founding principles.

Important Events of Prohibition

1914
World War I begins.

1790
American doctor and politician Benjamin Rush writes a pamphlet attacking hard liquor.

1893
The Anti-Saloon League is formed.

| 1750 | 1800 | 1850 | 1900 |

1850s
Several states briefly ban alcohol sales.

1890s
The Progressive movement, which views government and the legal system as necessary to improving life for the poor, has its beginnings.

1917
Congress passes the Eighteenth Amendment, making it a crime for Americans to sell, transport, or manufacture alcohol in most circumstances.

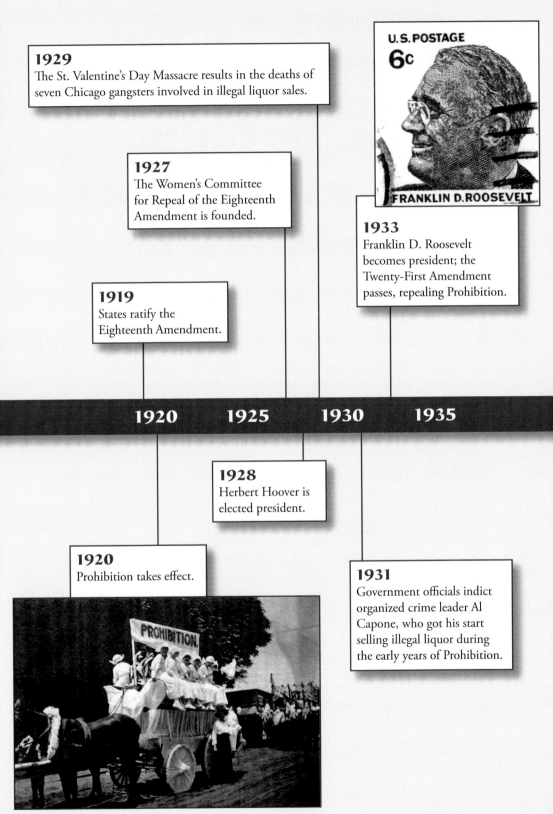

1929
The St. Valentine's Day Massacre results in the deaths of seven Chicago gangsters involved in illegal liquor sales.

1927
The Women's Committee for Repeal of the Eighteenth Amendment is founded.

U. S. POSTAGE
6¢
FRANKLIN D. ROOSEVELT

1933
Franklin D. Roosevelt becomes president; the Twenty-First Amendment passes, repealing Prohibition.

1919
States ratify the Eighteenth Amendment.

1920   1925   1930   1935

1928
Herbert Hoover is elected president.

1920
Prohibition takes effect.

1931
Government officials indict organized crime leader Al Capone, who got his start selling illegal liquor during the early years of Prohibition.

PROHIBITION

7

The Defining Characteristics of Prohibition

In 1919 the US government formally approved the Eighteenth Amendment to the Constitution. Known as the Prohibition amendment, the new measure made it illegal to sell, transport, or manufacture most forms of alcohol. The amendment was sparked by concerns that alcoholic beverages were immoral, along with worries about the negative social and physical effects of drinking. Supporters of Prohibition were delighted that it had been approved so quickly and easily. When Prohibition officially went into effect in 1920, these supporters confidently predicted a better, healthier, and less corrupt America in the years to come.

As sources of legal liquor dried up, drinking did drop off considerably. The best estimates available today suggest that consumption of alcohol decreased by about 70 percent in the first years of Prohibition. The drop cheered proponents of the new law, who also noted that alcohol-related disease, crime, and violence diminished correspondingly. However, the news was not all good for Prohibition's supporters. Though drinking was at historically low levels, even a 70 percent drop in consumption meant that Americans were still drinking millions upon millions of gallons of alcohol every year. The negative effects of alcohol on society and individual people, then, were not yet a thing of the past.

Americans continued to drink despite the new law for a variety of reasons. Some were physically and emotionally dependent on alcohol and could not give it up nearly as easily as Prohibition's supporters believed. Others enjoyed drinking in moderation. They agreed that drinking to excess caused significant social upheaval. Yet they did not agree that alcohol itself was to blame, and they saw no reason why they should give up their beer or whiskey because other people could not drink responsibly. And still others disliked the law for social and cultural reasons. These included professionals in large cities accustomed to their afternoon cocktails, working men in urban neighborhoods who often drank beer at nearby taverns, and recent immigrants from places with long traditions of alcohol use. Members of each of these groups continued to drink regardless of the Prohibition amendment.

Because liquor sales were now illegal, though, drinkers could no longer obtain their alcohol at legitimate stores or neighborhood bars. With these businesses shuttered, those who wanted to continue to drink were forced to buy alcohol illegally. Prohibition thus turned millions of otherwise law-abiding Americans into criminals overnight. As a result, many Americans took the laws in general less seriously, and they treated law enforcement officers with less respect than they had previously. By writing their concerns about drinking into law, Prohibition's advocates had assumed that all Americans would willingly obey the rules. As it turned out, that assumption was wrong.

Organized Crime

The situation soon grew more complicated. Recognizing an opportunity to make money, career criminals—and, in a few cases, ordinary citizens as well—hurried to provide illegal alcohol, known as moonshine or bootleg, to those who still drank. These outlaws set up illegal distilleries where they made whiskey or gin. They opened illegal saloons, sometimes known as speakeasies. They smuggled alcohol into the United States from Canada, the Caribbean, and elsewhere. The profits that could be made from illegal liquor sales were enormous, and soon organized gangs were competing with each other to control liquor distribution in cities and towns across the country.

Nor was law enforcement able to manage the rise in illegal alcohol. Though Congress and the states each set aside money to fight the

Government agents seize barrels of wine in New York City in 1921. The sale, transport, and manufacture of most forms of alcohol were banned under Prohibition, but that did not keep Americans from making, selling, buying, and drinking liquor, beer, and wine.

gangs, the funding was seldom sufficient to do the job. There were never enough agents to intercept liquor shipments, shut down the speakeasies, or raid the illegal distilleries. To make matters worse, organized crime rings routinely threatened and bribed the agents entrusted with enforcement, as well as prosecutors, judges, and jurors. Gangs therefore often conducted their business in full view of government officials, secure in the belief that they would not be arrested or convicted. In one of the great ironies of the twentieth century, a law designed to make America a less morally corrupt nation was causing a high level of political corruption.

Prohibition suffered from other problems too. The law contained a good many loopholes. There were exemptions for priests and rabbis, exemptions for alcohol used for medicinal purposes, exemptions for people with large private supplies of alcohol, and exemptions for alcohol used in manufacturing processes. Enterprising citizens exploited these loopholes to obtain alcohol for their own use—and, more often than not, for resale. Government revenues dropped when alcohol was outlawed. As a legal product, its manufacture and sale had once been taxed heavily; but now that it was an illegal substance, there was no way to collect taxes on it. Nor could Prohibition-era governments inspect the supply of liquor to make sure it was safe. Illegal alcohol sometimes included toxic substances that injured, sickened, and even killed thousands of people.

The Nation Abandons Prohibition

By the early 1930s, Americans had had enough. The tide of opinion had shifted. Over a decade of continued drinking had convinced millions of Americans that the Prohibitionists had overestimated how easy it would be to eliminate drinking. The widespread lawlessness, moreover, alarmed even former supporters of the legislation. It was becoming increasingly evident that Prohibition was not working—and would most probably never work. In late 1933 the country took the unprecedented step of passing another constitutional amendment designed specifically to overturn a previous one. Prohibition was no more.

Though the Prohibition era was short, and though from most perspectives it was a dismal failure, it had an important impact. It divided the country, pitting urban areas against rural areas, immigrant groups against the native born, moralists against those with a more pragmatic bent. In political debate, in the world of crime, and in several other ways its legacy continues today. Moreover, Prohibition lives on in popular culture and in the popular imagination as a time when gun-toting gangsters patrolled the streets of American cities, delivering bootleg beer to speakeasies while the police stood idly by. The Prohibition era was a colorful and fascinating time, with outsized personalities on both sides of the divide. It is well worth a look for that reason alone.

Chapter 1

What Conditions Led to Prohibition?

The Prohibition era represented the only time that the United States banned the sale and manufacture of alcohol altogether. But the roots of Prohibition lie much deeper in American history. Almost since the founding of the United States, people were expressing concern about the role of alcohol in American life. As the 1700s turned into the 1800s, the concerns slowly grew; and as the nineteenth century wore on, the chorus of voices opposing alcohol use in the United States became ever louder and more strident. Opponents of alcohol argued that it was the work of the devil, that it destroyed lives, homes, and families, and that it represented an enormous threat to American prosperity and the American way of life. Armed with facts and figures, appealing to religion and morality, and reasoning from science and logic, the anti-alcohol forces created one of America's most important social movements long before Prohibition was actually passed.

At the same time, throughout the nineteenth century—and into the twentieth as well—those who advocated against alcohol met with plenty of opposition. Many Americans liked to drink alcohol and saw drinking as a perfectly acceptable part of American culture and traditions. Those who argued in favor of alcohol rejected the notion that alcohol use carried significant social, economic, and moral costs, whether for individuals or for the nation, and they greatly resented the efforts of the antidrinking forces. As the nineteenth century wore on, the battle lines between these two groups became clearer, and the hostility between them began to grow. This tension set the stage for the later debate over Prohibition—and helped shape what Prohibition would become.

Early America

Alcohol has always had a major presence in American history. Indeed, drinking was a part of American culture long before the United States even existed. The *Mayflower,* which brought the Pilgrims to Massachusetts in 1620, carried not only colonists but also a large supply of beer; the *Arabella,* a ship that arrived in Massachusetts just a few years later, brought 10,000 gallons (37,854L) of wine from England to the thirsty colonists. During the 1600s and 1700s, colonists from New Hampshire to Georgia did their best to manufacture their own alcoholic drinks, brewing beer, distilling whiskey, and mashing apples into a beverage known as hard cider. Though the colonists did not always have the ingredients to produce exactly the same drinks they remembered from Europe, they were nonetheless resourceful—and willing to experiment. "We can make liquor to sweeten our lips," ran a ditty from early America, "of pumpkins, and parsnips, and walnut-tree chips."[1]

In most parts of the United States, alcoholic drinks became even more readily available during the nineteenth century. Farmers, particularly on the frontier, produced whiskey by fermenting their grain and then distilling it—that is, heating it to concentrate the alcohol. Rum, another distilled drink, was produced in bulk in New England from molasses and sugar imported from the Caribbean. Beer, with a lower-alcohol content than distilled liquors, was easy to make at home, and many people did just that. In the second half of the 1800s, moreover, the brewing of beer became a major industry, especially in midwestern cities such as St. Louis and Milwaukee. Wine, gin, and brandy—a distilled version of wine—were manufactured at home or in small factories throughout the nineteenth century. And anyone with access to an apple tree could, and often did, use the apples to make hard cider.

For many Americans, moreover, alcohol was a central part of life. Estimates suggest that the average American adult in 1820 consumed well over twice as much alcohol as the average American adult today. Part of the reason, oddly enough, had to do with health. Water supplies in early America, especially in the cities, were often unsafe. Water in wells and lakes could carry diseases such as cholera, an often fatal intestinal

and German immigrants discovered that the alcohol business—whether brewing beer or opening a tavern—could bring them money and status. Finally, drinking was often a reaction to the difficulties immigrants faced once in the United States. "Drink was a refuge from loneliness," notes a writer, describing the experiences of early Irish immigrants to America. "Displacement from rural Ireland to the major metropolises of the western world cannot have been easy."[5]

Alcohol Abuse

The constant presence of alcohol, however, had a dark side. In fact, alcohol abuse was a significant issue in America during the years before Prohibition. The problems seemed particularly acute among city dwellers, immigrants, and the poor. These groups led difficult lives under the best of circumstances. Not only did they lack money, but they also frequently lived in crowded housing, worked long hours in unhealthy conditions, and had little prospect of ever leading better lives. Alcohol was a refuge from these harsh realities of life—and as social critics of the nineteenth century saw it, a cause of the problems as well. "Forty percent of the distress among the poor," concluded a report from the 1880s, "is due to drunkenness."[6]

Indeed, drunks were a common sight in 1800s America. Virtually every community had at least one inhabitant—usually, though not always, a man—whose life had come to revolve entirely around drinking. These people were no longer able to work or to maintain a home; they had become, as one report put it, the "criminals in your penitentiaries, patients in your hospitals, lunatics in your asylums, and vagabonds in your streets."[7] Many had once been respectable citizens of their towns and villages, making their downfall seem even more tragic. A considerable number, moreover, were married and had children. Since women had few ways of supporting themselves, the descent of family men into alcoholism often sent their wives and children into poverty.

Another issue was the prevalence of bars, saloons, and other drinking establishments. As the nineteenth century wore on and society became more urbanized, these became more and more common in American

Mass Meetings

Antiliquor advocates of the mid-1800s often used mass meetings to spread their message. These meetings consisted mainly of speeches detailing the problems caused by liquor. Some speeches offered statistics to suggest the extent of the problem. Other speakers, convinced that Christianity required abstinence from alcohol, drew a link between God and the temperance movement. Still other speakers were reformed drinkers who offered personal testimony about their fall into drunkenness and their eventual recovery.

Mass meetings often included music and drama as well as lectures. A melodrama called *The Drunkard,* for example, told the story of a respectable young man brought to ruin by drink. In a typical scene the curtain opens to reveal the main character, now a habitual drunkard, "lying on [the] ground . . . clothes torn, eyes sunk and haggard, appearance horrible." The play does have a happy ending; the man is rescued by a kindly temperance advocate, renounces alcohol, and regains his reputation.

Audience members typically responded positively to these meetings. Temperance speakers were often excellent orators, and many felt especially energized by the notion that they were doing God's work. The musical and theatrical performances, by appealing directly to the emotions, had a particularly strong effect on audience members. Meetings usually culminated with an invitation for audience members to come forward and sign a pledge publicly renouncing liquor. At the most successful meetings, dozens of men would sign.

W.H. Smith, *The Drunkard; or, the Fallen Saved.* New York: Wm. Taylor, 1850, p. 48.

cities and towns. In 1876 Philadelphia had over eight thousand businesses that served drinks; late nineteenth-century Chicago had thirty times as many bars as churches. The bars, most of them open only to men, offered patrons a wide variety of alcoholic drinks. In an atmosphere where nearly everyone was drinking, many of them to excess, it was easy for customers to become intoxicated. Worse, saloons attracted criminals, prostitutes, and gamblers, thus introducing drinkers to other vices; a thoroughly inebriated man was not generally in a position to resist temptation. "The saloon was a blight and a public stench," sums up a historian. "It was dingy and dirty, a place of battered furniture, offensive smells, flyblown mirrors and glassware, appalling sanitary facilities."[8]

Violence was yet another problem. Alcohol lowers inhibitions and impairs judgment, and incidents of alcohol-fueled domestic violence were common in nineteenth-century America. One typical report from the late 1800s mentioned a Boston man who, "in a fit of drunken frenzy . . . dragged his wife up [a] dark staircase by the hair of her head, with the little puny five weeks' old baby in her arms, and flung them into the street."[9] Bar brawls were frequent; so were street fights involving men who had been drinking. When the only weapons used were fists, these fights sometimes resulted only in relatively minor injuries, such as broken noses and bruised ribs. But when knives and guns were involved—and they frequently were—fighters were often seriously injured or even killed.

The Temperance Movement

During colonial times, few people paid much attention to the problems caused by drink. But after the American Revolution, some influential thinkers began to question whether Americans were drinking too much. One of the first Americans to warn against the dangers of alcohol was a Philadelphian named Benjamin Rush. In addition to being involved in politics—he was one of the signers of the Declaration of Independence—Rush was a highly respected doctor. In 1790, concerned about the impact of alcohol on the nation, Rush wrote an influential pamphlet attacking the use of distilled drinks, or spirits. In the

Women and Temperance

During the 1800s most Americans considered it unseemly for women to become involved in political causes. There were occasional exceptions, though, and one of them was the temperance movement. Unlike political issues related to monetary policy, say, or debates over the best routes for railroads, temperance was acknowledged as one of the few controversies that directly affected the traditional woman's sphere of home and family. A woman whose husband drank excessively, after all, was in danger of losing her only means of support.

Since women's lives were so tightly bound to the issue of alcohol, women who weighed in against the problems of drink were accepted as activists. Indeed, many of the great temperance leaders of the late 1800s were women. Teacher and writer Frances Willard, for example, was the longtime president of the highly influential Women's Christian Temperance Union. Ellen Harmon White, a founder of the Seventh-Day Adventist Church, gave dozens of speeches on temperance. Susan B. Anthony, best known for her tireless advocacy of women's voting rights, was involved in temperance activities as well. Many, though not all, of these women eventually branched out into the discussion of other social and political issues, including religious freedom, racism, the right of women to vote, and more. In this way, the temperance movement served as a vital training ground for bringing women into the American political realm.

pamphlet Rush condemned the effects of excessive liquor on both the body and the mind. Spirits, he wrote, "impair the memory, debilitate the understanding, and pervert the moral faculties. . . . They produce not only falsehood [lies], but fraud, theft, uncleanliness, and murder."[10]

Rush did not condemn all forms of alcohol. His pamphlet did not concern itself with lower-alcohol beverages like beer, hard cider, and wine. Indeed, in addition to recommending that drinkers of hard liquor switch to pure water or coffee, Rush noted that fermented drinks could be acceptable substitutes for the harder liquors. "Wines generally inspire cheerfulness and good humour," Rush wrote approvingly; he even gave his readers directions for making their own beer. Still, Rush left no doubt that his preference would be for Americans to drink no alcohol at all. Most notably, he specified that the use of beer, wine, and cider should be reserved for those "who are unable to relish [the] simple beverage of nature"[11]—that is, water.

Soon, other early American figures were echoing Rush's disapproval of alcohol. In 1826, for example, Protestant minister Lyman Beecher delivered a series of sermons opposing the drinking of hard liquor. In these sermons Beecher noted the physical and mental effects of alcohol abuse, but he emphasized a different issue. As Beecher saw it, alcohol consumption was morally wrong, and it was steadily pushing the United States down a path that would inevitably lead to ethical bankruptcy. He believed that drink was destroying the nation—and, by extension, humanity. The answer, as he saw it, was temperance—the drinking of alcoholic beverages in moderation, and perhaps not at all. "Intemperance [excessive drinking] is the sin of our land," he thundered. "If anything shall defeat the hopes of the world . . . it is that river of fire, which is rolling through the land, destroying the vital air, and extending around an atmosphere of death."[12]

By the 1840s temperance had become an important movement with a growing number of supporters. Temperance societies formed across the country, dedicated to warning Americans of the problems caused by alcohol. Antiliquor advocates spread their message using statistics, personal testimony, and song. A popular song called "Father's a Drunkard and Mother Is Dead" told of the travails of Bessie, homeless and abandoned because her father could not or would not give up drinking. "God pity Bessie," the refrain exclaimed, "the Drunkard's lone child!"[13] Some antiliquor workers gathered in front of saloons to dissuade men from going inside. A Kansas woman named Carry Nation armed groups of women with hatchets and led them into local saloons, where they proceeded to break glasses, pour liquor on the floors, and chop up tables and chairs. "Smash, ladies, smash!,"[14] she reportedly shouted as surprised drinkers fled or cowered behind the bar.

Carry Nation (pictured with her trademark hatchet and bible) became the face of the temperance movement. Armed with hatchets, Nation and other movement members expressed their distaste for alcohol by smashing glasses, tables, and chairs at saloons.

"Moral Suasion for the Man Who Drinks"

As the nineteenth century wore on, the focus of temperance activists began to change. One of the changes involved the differences between types of alcoholic drinks. Temperance workers in the 1820s and early 1830s typically drew a distinction between lighter drinks, such as beer and wine, and harder liquors such as whiskey and rum. By the 1840s, however, most temperance advocates had changed their emphasis. Noting that it was not hard to get drunk on wine and beer, they were speaking out against all forms of alcohol. At the same time, the notion that small amounts of liquor might not be harmful came under attack. More and more, temperance advocates began criticizing virtually all use of alcohol, no matter how infrequent. As one report concluded, "There seems to be no safe line of distinction between the *moderate* and *immoderate* use of intoxicating drinks."[15]

The temperance movement underwent another important change as well. At first, advocates for the cause relied on encouragement to help people renounce alcohol. "Moral suasion [persuasion] for the man who drinks"[16] was the watchword for many of these activists. As time passed, however, it became increasingly apparent that mere persuasion was not especially effective. Despite their success in getting men to sign the temperance pledge, millions of men were far from willing to give up alcohol—and many who did sign proved to be backsliders who soon returned to their drinking ways. By the late 1840s, many temperance advocates were ready to give up on encouragement as their primary strategy for combating alcohol.

Instead, many temperance advocates began trying a more sweeping and political approach: banning alcohol outright. Unfortunately for them, their efforts were decidedly mixed. Though many counties and towns began banning alcohol beginning in the 1850s, efforts for more sweeping legislation stalled. Several states passed laws forbidding the manufacture and sale of alcohol, but these statewide laws proved unpopular. Americans of the mid-nineteenth century tended to oppose government intervention in their lives. Whether a person chose to drink, in popular opinion, was the business of that person alone—not the business of the government. Consequently, many Americans, including some who opposed alcohol in general, were suspicious of any attempt to legislate against it. "The drink habit is personal," admitted one temperance advocate, "and involves the liberty of the individual."[17] Most statewide prohibitions against alcohol, then, were repealed by the end of the Civil War.

The Progressives and the Law

For a time, the temperance movement stalled. Then, in the 1890s, a new social movement began to develop in the United States. Known as Progressivism, this movement had several goals, among them a desire to

Ratification of the Eighteenth Amendment, by State

In the 1890s antiliquor forces got a boost from the Progressive movement, which successfully argued that the government could make and enforce laws for the greater good. The temperance movement adopted this rationale when it argued that a government ban on alcohol would help fix troubling social problems. As persuasive as this argument seemed at the time, ratification of the Eighteenth Amendment banning the manufacture and sale of alcohol took several years.

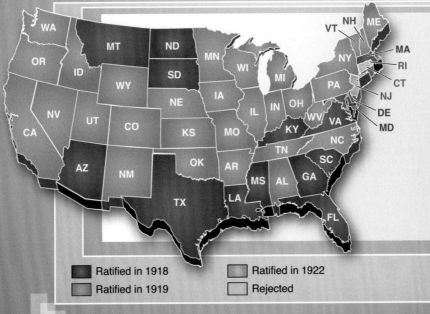

- Ratified in 1918
- Ratified in 1919
- Ratified in 1922
- Rejected

improve the lives of the poor. Unlike previous groups with similar purposes, however, the Progressives wasted little time appealing to factory owners to raise wages or trying to persuade slumlords to provide running water for every tenant. The Progressives were too cynical to believe that these strategies would work. As a result, they turned instead to the legal system for a remedy. They lobbied for a variety of laws that would force the government and the upper class to treat the poor more fairly.

The Progressives were not able to get all their proposed laws passed, and even the laws that were approved were often less effective than the movement's leaders hoped. Enforcement was often difficult too. Nonetheless, the Progressives successfully changed the way Americans thought about government. During the early twentieth century the lines between what was private and what was public were becoming blurred. While the great majority of Americans had once believed that factory owners or landlords could do whatever they pleased with their property, more and more were coming to accept that the people, in the form of the government, might have a say in these issues as well. And if the government could make and enforce laws mandating minimum size for apartments, say, for the greater good, then surely the government could ban alcohol for the same reason.

The time, then, was right for the temperance movement to push forward. As the twentieth century dawned, the antiliquor forces were reinvigorated. With their emphasis on fixing social problems through government action, the Progressives had paved the way for the temperance activists to become not simply temperance workers but Prohibitionists—people advocating for a total legal ban on alcohol. The temperance movement's moral and practical opposition to alcohol had now taken a different tack. Ready for a struggle, assured in their belief that their cause was just, and certain that they would ultimately prevail, anti-alcohol leaders prepared to battle for their new goal.

Chapter 2

Prohibition Begins

"The day of deliverance from the saloon is near,"[18] one Iowa newspaper editorialized in 1914. After many years of struggling against liquor, the anti-alcohol forces were at last approaching their objective. Between 1890 and the mid-1910s—thanks in part to their dogged determination and in part to their willingness to learn from the Progressive movement and its emphasis on changing the laws to change behavior—the temperance movement achieved remarkable success in a very short period of time. In January 1920, when Prohibition officially went into effect, the movement had accomplished something that few other American social movements, past or present, could claim: It had changed the US Constitution, the fundamental document on which the laws of the country are based.

But although the movement had swept easily to victory, the first months and years of Prohibition were problematic. From issues with enforcement to questions of fairness, from troublesome loopholes in the law to the reality that drinking was not quick to disappear, the amendment was proving to be less than perfect. From the vantage point of 1920, 1921, or even 1922, it was understandable that supporters of the new laws might overlook the amendment's flaws in favor of concentrating solely on its virtues—and might insist, if pushed, that with time any small complications would vanish. But in hindsight, the amendment was much less effective than ardent Prohibitionists cared to admit. Indeed, despite the excitement and the optimism that surrounded its passage, the amendment might have been doomed from the start.

The Anti-Saloon League

The push toward Prohibition began in earnest with the formation in 1893 of a group called the Anti-Saloon League. Like the burgeoning Progressive movement of the time, the Anti-Saloon League had a legislative focus from its start. Representatives of the organization met regularly with elected leaders to explain why alcohol should be banned. Members of the group also utilized lobbying techniques that would not be out of place in today's political world. In particular, they reminded legislators and other officials that those who opposed their agenda did so at considerable risk to their political careers. Privately, and publicly when necessary, the organization informed lawmakers that it would use its political muscle to defeat legislators who voted against limitations on liquor.

It was not an empty threat. In 1904 Ohio governor Myron Herrick, a Republican, successfully lobbied the state legislature to defeat a bill that the Anti-Saloon League supported. Anti-alcohol Republicans, outraged by the governor's actions, urged party leaders not to nominate Herrick for another term as governor the following year. They were ignored, however, and Herrick was chosen as the Republican candidate. At this point the Anti-Saloon League swung into action. Though Herrick had won election easily in 1901, this election was a different story. "While the [other] candidates of the Republican state ticket [were] elected by the normal majority," Anti-Saloon League member Ernest Cherrington crowed, "there was one exception . . . Governor Herrick, who went down to defeat before an avalanche of Christian protests."[19]

Across the United States, politicians took note. From 1904 to 1914, spearheaded by the Anti-Saloon League and its political allies, state and county legislators passed dozens of new laws with the goal of limiting the sale of alcohol. Tennessee, for example, passed a law that forced the closure of saloons in nearly all the state's counties. South Dakota gave police the power to confiscate liquor being sold without a license, and it instituted what Cherrington described as "several other splendid restrictive temperance measures"[20] as well. Connecticut

Jack London and Prohibition

Author and journalist Jack London is probably best known today for his novels *The Call of the Wild* and *White Fang*, each of which deals with adventure in the frozen North. London's own life was something of an adventure as well. Besides being a writer, he was at various times an oyster fisherman, a gold miner, and a tramp. He traveled frequently, sometimes working as a deckhand on a ship to pay for his passage. London's health was seldom good, and he often lived close to the edge of financial and emotional ruin.

London was also a heavy drinker. By the definitions of today, London would no doubt have qualified as an alcoholic. He was dependent on liquor and unable to stop drinking despite the physical and mental damage it did. Nonetheless, London frequently wished that he could give up alcohol, and this desire led him to support Prohibition. As he wrote in an autobiographical account of his relationship with liquor, he thought that he might finally be able to stop drinking in a time "when no one else drinks and when no drink is obtainable."

However, London never had the chance to find out whether Prohibition would have halted his difficulties with alcohol. He died in 1916, at the age of forty, several years before the new law went into effect. Though the cause of his death is unclear, most authorities agree that alcohol abuse played a role in his early demise.

Quoted in Daniel Okrent, *Last Call.* New York: Scribner, 2010, p. 63.

barred pharmacists from dispensing alcohol—often used medicinally at the time—unless the customer had a valid prescription. Georgia provided money and resources to make sure that anti-alcohol laws already on the books were enforced.

State and local legislators were not the only people with a new enthusiasm for temperance measures. The general public, too, was increasingly tiring of the troubles caused by alcohol and increasingly willing to back new laws against drinking. Indeed, one of the Anti-Saloon League's strategies was to convince legislators to put anti-alcohol laws to a public vote. Most often these votes took place on the county, town, or village level; voters were asked whether to outlaw bars within this political unit, or, in the political slang of the day, to make the territory dry. By 1910 most of these elections were resulting in victories for temperance forces. In hundreds of counties and cities across the nation, voters approved measures that banned saloons, outlawed the manufacture of liquor, or made it a felony to bring alcohol into a dry community.

Not every American of the time supported these laws. Liquor manufacturers, bar owners, and ordinary drinkers fought hard against the laws of the early 1900s, and they did manage to prevent a few from going into effect. In 1910, for example, anti-alcohol laws on the ballot failed in both Florida and Oregon. The following year, despite intense lobbying by the Anti-Saloon League, Nebraska's legislature refused to allow counties to vote themselves dry. Still, the trend was clear. The *wets*—those who believed that alcohol should be easily available—were increasingly on the defensive, watching in dismay as the *drys*, or those who wanted to abolish alcohol, gained in stature and strength. The drys, in turn, were rapidly growing more and more confident. "It is going to be a real fight," temperance worker William Anderson concluded, "and we won't admit to defeat."[21]

Changing the Constitution

In 1917 it seemed that the temperance movement's time had come. That fall, temperance leaders introduced a constitutional amendment to prohibit the manufacture and sale of alcohol within the United States. The first step in making this amendment law was for both houses of Congress to approve it, with at least two thirds of the members of each house voting in favor. That was not difficult. Both the

Authorities empty confiscated barrels of beer in the 1920s. The Volstead Act gave teeth to Prohibition by authorizing money and manpower for the enforcement of the alcohol ban.

House and Senate easily approved the measure that December. In the House, the vote was 282 in favor and 128 opposed, with a clear majority of representatives from both political parties voting for the bill. In the Senate, the vote was even more lopsided: just seven senators opposed the measure.

Proliquor forces loudly voiced their disapproval of Congress and its vote. Many charged senators and representatives with cowardice in the face of the antiliquor lobby's strength. "If the vote could have been by secret ballot it is doubtful if there would have been a majority of either house,"[22] complained journalist Arthur Wallace Dunn, expressing his belief that many members of Congress were personally opposed to the law but feared the consequences of offending the drys by voting against it. Next, the measure went to the states, where three-quarters

World War I

In 1914 World War I broke out in Europe, pitting Germany and its allies against a group of countries that included Great Britain, France, and Russia. In 1917 the United States joined the conflict on the British side. The entrance into the war strengthened the drive toward Prohibition. One reason was ethnic prejudice, particularly against the German Americans who dominated the beer industry. Many Americans viewed brewers as anti-American, or at least not American enough, and were reluctant to spend their money on "German" products. Beer sales quickly tailed off when America formally entered the fighting.

The needs of wartime made a difference too. When the nation was at war, the consequences of excessive drinking were magnified. Workers who had been drinking before beginning their shifts in a factory, for example, made more mistakes than those who reported to work sober. That was a problem if the mistake led to a defective pair of shoes. It was a disaster, however, if it led to the manufacture of cannons that would not fire.

Finally, World War I was a time of strict rationing, when consumption of everything from food to fuel was limited. Americans accordingly questioned why grain should be used for alcohol production at a time of food shortages. "How can we justify the making of any part of our breadstuffs into intoxicating liquor," asked politician William Jennings Bryan, "when men are crying out for bread?" The war made abstinence from liquor patriotic—and thereby more acceptable to millions of Americans.

Quoted in Daniel Okrent, *Last Call.* New York: Scribner, 2010, p. 99.

of the legislatures—thirty-six of the forty-eight in existence at the time—needed to ratify, or approve, the amendment in order to make it official. That proved easy as well, with the thirty-sixth state ratifying the amendment in January 1919. The new law would go into effect on January 16, 1920—exactly one year from the date of ratification.

The process was not quite complete. Members of the Anti-Saloon League had learned from earlier mistakes made by temperance advocates. In their opinion, previous attempts to legislate against alcohol had failed partly because there was no mechanism for enforcing the law. Accordingly, Congress passed a bill called the Volstead Act, which allowed the federal government to devote money and officials to arrest and punish those who broke the law. With the approval of the Volstead Act, advocates of the new law were sure they had done everything right. "This law will be obeyed in cities, large and small, and in villages," promised John Kramer, the nation's first commissioner in charge of enforcing Prohibition, "and where it is not obeyed it will be enforced. . . . We shall see that [liquor] is not manufactured. Nor sold, nor given away, nor hauled in anything on the surface of the earth or under the earth or in the air."[23]

Complications and Loopholes

At first glance the amendment was clear, simple, and straightforward; there could be little debate about what it meant or what it implied. As the first section put it, the amendment simply forbade "the manufacture, sale, or transportation of intoxicating liquors within . . . the United States"[24] and its territories. The amendment also specifically banned Americans from importing alcoholic drinks from abroad. This was a particular concern given the long borders the United States shared with Mexico and Canada, in addition to dozens of US seaports that attracted cargo ships from all over the world.

The simplicity of the amendment's wording masked some significant flaws with the wording of the Volstead Act—and what it did and did not permit. Most obviously, although Americans could no longer make or sell alcohol, the Volstead Act did not ban *drinking* beer, whiskey, or indeed anything else. As long as they had purchased it before January 16, 1920, Americans were allowed to consume all the alcohol they wanted. Some Prohibitionists opposed this exception, arguing that Prohibition should mean a complete ban on drinking regardless of when the liquor had originally been purchased. But they were overruled, in part because many political leaders—including a number who had voted for Prohibition—owned extensive private stocks of liquor that they did not wish to see wasted. The exemption for drinking, while perhaps necessary to ensure passage of the amendment, was nonetheless controversial. It seemed to many observers, wets and drys alike, as not consistent with the spirit of the amendment.

Similarly, though a quick reading of the amendment suggested that all forms of alcohol were to be banned, that was not the case. Wine is an important part of religious ritual in Judaism and several branches of Christianity; thus, the Volstead Act provided partial exemptions from the new law for rabbis and priests. Alcohol is also used in a variety of manufacturing processes, so the Volstead Act included exemptions for factories that required alcohol for this purpose. Finally, since alcohol was believed to have medicinal uses, pharmacists could continue to dispense medications containing alcohol to patients with valid prescriptions. The Volstead Act specified that "not more than a pint of spirituous liquor"[25] could be taken medicinally by any person during a ten-day period, but it said nothing about beer or wine. These loopholes might have been necessary to get the Volstead Act passed, but they had the effect of allowing the manufacture of alcohol to continue—in defiance of what the amendment seemed to suggest.

There were other loopholes too. One involved a drink called near beer. Near beer is made to taste like beer, but has little or no alcohol content. Because the amount of alcohol in near beer was so low, the Volstead Act ruled that it could continue to be made and sold even during Prohibition. However, as historian Frederick Lewis Allen writes, "The only way to manufacture near-beer was to brew real beer and then remove the alcohol from it"[26]—a process that seemed ripe for abuse. And in order to avoid offending rural voters who enjoyed hard cider, the authors of the Volstead Act permitted farmers to ferment fruit juices legally. "No [farmer] would be denied the barrel by the homestead door," writes historian Daniel Okrent, "the jug stashed in a corner of the field, the comforting warmth on cold country nights."[27]

Perhaps the biggest issue of all, though, was money. While Congress was happy to pass the Volstead Act, it was reluctant to authorize sufficient funds for its enforcement. When Prohibition first went into effect, for example, the federal government provided just 1,520 officers to enforce the law—an average of only about thirty per state and clearly not enough to close down all saloons, raid all distilleries, and arrest all those who tried to smuggle in alcohol from outside the country. Moreover, the salaries of these agents were small, which made some observers question whether the government was attracting agents who were truly dedicated, intelligent, and incorruptible. Looking back, Allen writes, the answer should have been obvious: Anyone who genuinely believed that enforcement was exclusively in the hands of honest, capable men "would be ready to believe also in Santa Claus, perpetual motion, and pixies."[28]

Positive Signs

Despite the potential issues presented by the new amendment, January 16, 1920, was a wonderful day for the drys. "Reign of Demon Rum Now Ended,"[29] read the headline on a story in an Indiana newspaper, one of many with similar sentiments to appear that day in papers around the country. An Anti-Saloon League press release promised "an era of clear thinking and clean living!"[30] Others agreed. "The slums will soon be only a memory," proclaimed Billy Sunday, a retired baseball player and one-time heavy drinker who had become an antiliquor crusader. "Hell will be forever for rent."[31] Drys held mock funerals for alcohol, most of them observed by large and approving audiences. In some cities enthusiastic Anti-Saloon League members imitated Carry Nation's infamous act of hacking barrels of beer and wine to bits and letting the alcohol spill onto the streets.

And in the first weeks and months of Prohibition, the drys could hardly have been happier. As they saw it, Prohibition was working beautifully. Supporters trotted out anecdotes to demonstrate the effectiveness of the new law—not just in preventing people from drinking but also in leading them to a new and better way of life. Everyone, it seemed, was acquainted with a man saving the money that once had gone to the saloonkeeper or a woman whose husband had sobered up and found a respectable job. "We were all elated by the marked decrease in so-called disorderly conduct,"[32] wrote social reformer Jane Addams, who ran a settlement house, or community center, in a downtrodden part of Chicago.

The drys also cited statistical evidence to support their claim that Prohibition was working. In 1920, they pointed out, the death rate from alcohol abuse was less than it had been in previous years. And, as leaders such as Billy Sunday had predicted, several cities shuttered some of their jails. The drys noted, too, that sales of nonalcoholic drinks, such as milk and fruit juice, were rising sharply. They quoted studies, moreover, indicating that drinking had largely disappeared; one congressman claimed that 85 percent of drinkers had given up alcohol completely in the first year of Prohibition. Finally, Prohibitionists pointed to the successes of law enforcement, citing well-publicized cases early in 1920 in which police forces shut down illegal saloons and broke up liquor-smuggling gangs. The few who tried to break the law, Prohibitionists stated, would very shortly be dissuaded from doing so.

In other ways, too, the signs were positive. Some observers had worried that the economy would suffer as the country adjusted to an existence without alcohol, but that did not seem to be a significant issue. For example, though breweries and distilleries had been forced to stop making alcohol, many were successfully being retooled to produce other goods. Some wineries turned to the manufacture of grape juice. A Detroit brewery began making and selling ice cream; a brewery in St. Louis started producing goods as varied as trolley cars and cereal. The exemption for near beer also helped keep some of the breweries in business. These new products were not as lucrative for the factory owners as the liquor trade had been. Even so, many factories were able to derive enough income from juice or cereal to keep their gates open and continue to provide income for their owners—and jobs for the people in their neighborhoods.

Flouting the Law

Still, those who paid close attention recognized that Prohibition was not working quite as advertised. The exemption for private stocks of alcohol, for example, proved vexing. Many drys were appalled that Warren Harding, who had been elected president in 1920, not only took his personal liquor supply to the White House but also drank from it liberally, even serving alcohol at some state dinners. Harding was setting a terrible example, they complained. The president, of all people, should lead the way for Americans by never touching liquor. Some observers

Residents of rural Tennessee boil sorghum for making moonshine in the late 1920s. Many Americans defied Prohibition by building backyard stills and basement breweries and then selling whatever product they did not consume.

were uncomfortable with the exemption for another reason: it favored the rich over the poor. Only the wealthy could afford to buy enormous quantities of liquor before Prohibition took effect. The result was that while the rich could continue to enjoy alcohol legally, the poor could not.

There were other issues too. The most realistic of the drys admitted, at least in private, that drinking had not been cut by nearly as much as the movement's staunchest advocates believed. One reason was that Americans were proving highly creative in finding ways to get around Prohibition. Many drinkers, for example, constructed backyard stills and basement breweries. These operations were too small to attract the attention of the authorities, but they were large enough to allow the owners to drink all they wanted with little fear of arrest. Better yet, many people found that they could make money selling the excess alcohol they made. "A commercial still could be set up for five hundred dollars," writes Allen, "which would produce fifty or a hundred highly remunerative gallons a day."[33]

Home distilleries were a problem, but smuggling alcohol in from foreign countries was a much bigger one. Residents of border towns and police officers alike knew that even in the early days of Prohibition, plenty of liquor was flowing into the country illegally. The head of the US Customs Service told Congress in late 1920 that a staggering amount of alcohol was entering the United States from Canada; furthermore, he admitted that his forces had been able to capture almost none of it. A Michigan newspaper, highlighting the problem for its readers in late 1921, referred to "the ease and comparative safety"[34] of smuggling and explained that the custom was growing rapidly. Like the flouting of the law by those who set up basement distilleries, the pervasiveness of smuggling suggested that there were some significant problems with Prohibition.

Bars too continued to flourish, especially in urban areas. Less than a year after Prohibition took effect, many observers reported, illegal saloons were operating in nearly every significant American city. Though occasional raids did shut them down briefly, others usually popped up to take their place. The loopholes written into the law were proving equally troublesome. Pharmacies, for example, were often willing to provide alcohol for customers—even those who did not have a doctor's prescription. Asked to obtain a drink for a visitor to his city, for example, a young Tennessean named Ralph McGill simply went to a nearby drugstore and placed an order. The only concession to the law, McGill reported afterward, was the label on the bottle, which bore the name of a nonalcoholic medication.

A Hollow Victory?

Despite these warning signs, however, the drys continued to insist throughout the early 1920s that Prohibition was going well. Drinking was down, they argued again and again, productivity was up, and the police forces hired to uphold the law were doing their jobs. The drys dismissed stories of widespread smuggling, home stills, and illegal saloons as isolated incidents, exaggerations, or outright lies. They had reason for their smugness. After all, they had won the battle: Prohibition, which the drys called "the greatest piece of moral legislation in the history of the world,"[35] was now enshrined in the Constitution. But though the forces of Prohibition had earned the victory, it remained to be seen how long that victory would last.

Chapter 3

Organized Crime and Law Enforcement

Of all the characteristics of the Prohibition era, the one that stands out most to Americans today is probably crime. The criminal activities of the Prohibition years have long fascinated authors, artists, and film directors. Movies, books, and other creative works set in the 1920s often focus on organized gangs of criminals who broke the law by providing liquor to thirsty Americans—and on the government agents who tried to stop them. Classic movies, such as *The Untouchables, Scarface,* and *Once Upon a Time in America,* are good examples of the film industry's attraction to this aspect of Prohibition. Likewise, F. Scott Fitzgerald's novel *The Great Gatsby* is one of many set against a backdrop of crime in the Prohibition era.

Like most fictional works that are based on real events, these books and movies do not always adhere strictly to the truth. Mob activities were not quite so dramatic as they may appear in books and movies about the 1920s, and law enforcement officials were not nearly as daring in their pursuit of mobsters as writers and directors have made them out to be. Nonetheless, the creative works that are founded on the criminal activities of Prohibition do not embellish the facts beyond recognition. Crime was truly a major aspect of the Prohibition era: important, dramatic, and central to the story of the time.

The Rise in Crime

The coming of Prohibition unquestionably spurred a jump in criminal activity. In part this was simply a result of criminalizing behaviors that had once been perfectly legal. In December 1919 residents of a wet county or state who bought a drink in a saloon or sold a bottle of beer were adhering to the law. The same activity just two months later, however, made them lawbreakers, subject to arrest, trial, and imprisonment. If about 70 percent of American drinkers gave up alcohol completely after Prohibition was passed—a figure that researchers today agree seems reasonably accurate—then millions of former alcohol users continued to indulge. And while some of those drank legally, using private stocks or manufacturing hard cider at home, most did not. In this way, millions of Americans became criminals overnight—not because their behavior had changed, but rather because the law had been redefined.

However, crime rose in another, more significant way as well. Though the new amendment had banned alcohol in nearly all circumstances, many Americans recognized that enforcement might prove extremely difficult. One reason was the addictive power that alcohol has over many people. While ardent Prohibitionists assured themselves that even the most hopelessly addicted Americans would sober up once all legal sources of liquor were removed, more thoughtful observers were less convinced. They feared that alcoholics would do whatever they could to make sure their supply of liquor continued without interruption. Law or no law, they would still demand alcoholic drinks.

Similarly, many Americans who enjoyed the taste of beer, wine, or whiskey were deeply unhappy with the new law. For quite a few of these citizens, drinking was an important part of their cultural heritage and civic life. Business colleagues sealed deals over a friendly drink; working men went to bars as a refuge from the difficulties of everyday life; families celebrated weddings and holidays with food, conviviality, and liquor. From the cocktails served at fancy hotel dining rooms to the low-priced gin and beer available at corner bars in small towns, alcohol was more than just a drink: It represented pleasure, sociability, and tradition. What with those who drank because they were addicted and those who drank because they wanted to, it seemed likely that millions of Americans would still demand alcohol, even after Prohibition became a part of the Constitution. And if they could not obtain alcohol legally, they would probably obtain it in some other way.

Bootlegging

There was precedent for this. Before Prohibition, states and counties that had forbidden the sale of alcohol were rarely successful in stamping it out completely. Even in the driest of dry territories, most communities had at least a few citizens who ignored the law and continued to drink. They obtained their alcohol from so-called bootleggers or rumrunners—small-time criminals who manufactured liquor illegally or brought it in from places where laws did not forbid alcohol sales. The bootleggers—the name is said to come from the tendency of smugglers to conceal bottles of liquor in their boots—were risking arrest, of course. But they charged and collected high prices to offset the dangers. A customer with a taste for alcohol, reported one Texas newspaper, "will pay liberally for any kind of whisky or kindred drink that he can obtain." Thus, the article concluded, "the bootlegger has a big profit on all his sales."[36]

Now, with the passage of nationwide Prohibition, the possible profits for bootlegging had soared. For hundreds of small-time criminals— and many otherwise law-abiding citizens—this presented a wonderful opportunity. By manufacturing liquor illegally or by importing it from elsewhere, an enterprising lawbreaker could sell to eager drinkers at almost any price he chose. Tempted by the prospect of extra income, farmers opened illegal distilleries and made whiskey to sell at a high return. Laborers who lived along the nation's borders gave up their jobs for the more lucrative work of smuggling alcohol into the country. And men who had worked in now-shuttered saloons helped slake the nation's thirst by opening illegal bars, known as speakeasies.

It soon became evident just how much money could be made from illegal liquor. "In the 13 months I have been in business," reported a bootlegger in 1921, "I have delivered to my customers . . . 1000 dozen

Florida bootleggers prepare to move their stash of alcohol during Prohibition. Bootleggers earned healthy profits on the sale of illicit liquor, beer, and wine.

quarts of whisky and gin at an average price of $120 per dozen. My profits averaged $30 a case, or $3.50 a quart." The bootlegger's best customer, he noted, was a wealthy businessman who was a particularly important source of cash. "Only recently . . . I delivered to his house $5400 worth of liquor," the bootlegger explained. "He paid me in cash. My profit was $1800."[37] That single day's profit was greater than the average annual salary of a Prohibition agent. It was no wonder that many Americans, even those who had always obeyed the law, found bootlegging attractive.

Thoughtful government officials correctly predicted that bootlegging might be an issue at the beginning of Prohibition. What they did not anticipate was how long it would last. The demand for liquor turned out to be nearly inexhaustible, and smugglers and bootleggers were happy to fill the need. In many places, especially in large urban areas, selling bootleg liquor became commonplace. In New York City,

George Remus and the Circle

Several criminal figures of the 1920s had worked in the legitimate business world. George Remus, who ran pharmacies in Chicago before becoming an attorney, was a notable example. Remus was a highly successful lawyer, earning an estimated fifty thousand dollars a year. It was not enough for him, however, and after Prohibition was passed Remus decided to turn to bootlegging instead.

Leaving the legal field, he moved from Chicago to Cincinnati, which was near most of America's whiskey distilleries. Many of these plants had closed during Prohibition, but some still manufactured and sold so-called bonded liquor, which was used for medicinal purposes. Remus soon developed a scheme that he called "the Circle." He bought as many distilleries as he could and used loopholes in the Volstead Act to sell the liquor—to himself. This part of the operation was perfectly legal. However, Remus then assigned his gang members to hijack the liquor as it was being transported. That let him sell the hijacked liquor at far higher prices than it would have fetched at a pharmacy. The hijacking was illegal—even if Remus was stealing liquor that rightfully belonged to him.

The system was effective: In just three years Remus made $40 million. But authorities eventually caught up with him. In 1925 he was arrested, convicted on several thousand counts of violating the Volstead Act, and sent to prison for two years. After his release he learned that his wife, Imogene, had begun an affair with a Prohibition agent and had hidden many of his assets so he could not access them. Enraged, he shot and killed Imogene after running her taxicab off the road, but he pleaded insanity and was given a light sentence. He died in 1952.

police stopped a hearse and discovered that it was transporting neither coffins nor corpses but sixty cases of liquor. In Detroit a steady stream of boats carried alcohol across the river that separated the city from Canada. For visitors to San Francisco, Philadelphia, St. Louis, and many other cities, getting a drink was as simple as asking for directions. "Walk right in and tell the man at the bar that Charley sent you," a New York waiter advised a traveler after pointing him to a nearby speakeasy. "He'll fix you up."[38]

With demand as high as it was, bootlegging rapidly became a major industry. Anticipating even more revenue, small-time smugglers expanded their operations. "My business has grown," boasted a smuggler who had gotten his start in bootlegging with a car, a small bankroll, and little else. "[Now] I have three fast automobiles and I employ drivers. The most reputable men in town are my regular customers and they are constantly sending me new buyers."[39] Asked to estimate the total value of his assets—cars, liquor, and cash on hand—this man claimed to have a net worth of ten thousand dollars, an impressive sum for the era. And business leaders who had once been involved in the legitimate alcohol trade joined the party as well. Canadian liquor manufacturer Sam Bronfman, for example, made an estimated four hundred thousand dollars a month smuggling alcohol into Minnesota from his base in central Canada.

Crime Rings

The sky-high profit potential of bootlegging, however, attracted not just newcomers to crime; it attracted seasoned criminals as well. Before Prohibition, there had been many crime rings in America—loosely organized groups of criminals who were involved in illegal activities such as prostitution and extortion. With the passage of Prohibition, many of these groups moved into bootlegging as well. Al Capone, one of Chicago's most famous gangsters, was just one example. The income from his illegal liquor sales was staggering. By the mid-1920s Capone's gang was earning $60 million a year from alcohol alone. When others chastened him for engaging in illegal activity, Capone had a ready response:

"I make my money," he is said to have explained, "by supplying a public demand."[40]

Other crime rings, hoping to share in the sudden prosperity, likewise entered the bootlegging business. The Bug and Meyer Mob, led by the notorious criminals Bugsy Siegel and Meyer Lansky, provided liquor to the people of New York City. In Philadelphia alcohol was sold by members of gangs led by men such as Maxie "Boo Boo" Hoff and Danny O'Leary. Rumrunning in Detroit, the leading port of entry for Canadian alcohol during Prohibition, was dominated by a gang known as the Purples. Mobs also set up shop in Denver, New Orleans, Baltimore, and other cities, opening speakeasies, setting up illegal distilleries, and shipping alcohol wherever there was a demand for it.

The rise of the gangs helped make bootlegging more organized and more profitable. The gangs were often led by shrewd businessmen who understood how to make money, and mob functionaries made the manufacture and transportation of illegal liquor more reliable and more efficient. Several gangs set up offshore operations in places like the Bahamas or Central America, for instance, where manufacturing alcohol was still legal and where US officials had no authority; then they smuggled the bootleg liquor ashore. In one year alone, nearly 2 million gallons (7.6 million L) of liquor came into the United States from a tiny French-owned island off Canada's Atlantic coast. "The history of the prohibition years," writes historian Elizabeth Stevenson, "[is] a history of increased efficiency in management by the gangs."[41]

Gangs and Violence

Inevitably, however, the gangs' desire to make money brought them into conflict with one another. Few gangs were content to earn hundreds of thousands of dollars a year when millions were there for the taking. As a result, they were unwilling to settle for less than a full share of the market. Thus, gangs frequently tried to take over each other's territory. In Detroit, for instance, the Purples constantly clashed with the Licavoli Squad and others for control of the liquor trade. Capone likewise fought off other mobsters who wanted to take market share from him in Chicago, and the Philadelphia gangs vied with one another to dominate certain sections of the city.

The gangs' great strength was not brains, however, but brawn. Most gangsters were violent men more interested in increasing market share by smashing their rivals' heads than by lowering prices or providing

The Birger Gang of southern Illinois (pictured in 1924) did a thriving business in bootleg liquor, roadhouses, and stolen cars until a feud erupted into a full-scale gang war that resulted in at least ten deaths. With rising profits at stake, gang violence increased.

better quality liquor. In Detroit, for instance, the Purples got their start in the liquor business by hijacking alcohol owned by other gangs. "Their methods were often brutal," reads a modern account. "Anyone landing liquor along the Detroit waterfront had to be armed and prepared to fight to the death, as it was common practice for the Purples to steal a load of liquor and shoot whoever was with it."[42] Similarly, in just four years, Chicago saw 135 gang killings, most connected to the distribution of liquor. Historian Frederick Lewis Allen called it "an epidemic of killings as no modern city had ever before seen."[43]

The violence of these gangs led to some especially memorable—and horrifying—episodes. Foremost among these was the St. Valentine's Day Massacre of February 14, 1929. That morning, some of Capone's gangsters entered a Chicago garage that served as the headquarters of a rival mob. Pretending to be police officers, Capone's men disarmed the seven mobsters inside—and then mowed them down with machine guns. "It was the most gruesome thing I ever hope to see in all my life," reported an eyewitness. "Their heads and bodies [were] virtually riddled with bullets."[44] The level of violence in this event was appalling—but not unique.

The Police

In contrast to the risk posed by other gangsters, bootleggers had little to fear from the police. Part of the reason, at least in some places, was cultural. In New York City, for instance, quite a few policemen were frequent drinkers themselves and saw little reason to uphold the law. "Many officers simply refused to see drinking as an offense worthy of their attention,"[45] sums up historian Michael Lerner. A much more compelling reason, however, was money, which bootleggers had and police typically did not. Many officers charged with preventing the movement of illegal liquor were happy to receive bribes from bootleggers in exchange for leaving them alone. That was true of police chiefs as well as rank-and-file patrol officers. "The local police captain had the reputation of being easy to deal with,"[46] Jane Addams wrote delicately, explaining why so many bootleggers sought out her Chicago neighborhood.

Once corrupted, police officers could keep bootleggers out of jail, but the largest gangs set their sights higher. Outfits such as the Bug and Meyer Mob in New York City bribed judges, mayors, and even governors in addition to law enforcement agents. Al Capone wielded so much influence over the elected officials of a Chicago suburb that he essentially ran the town. Elsewhere, judges obediently threw out cases against rumrunners regardless of the evidence against them. In Philadelphia, Boo Boo Hoff spent $2 million a year bribing police officers and more buying off congressmen, federal agents, and other key figures. Career military officer Smedley Butler, sent to Philadelphia to clean up the mess, found the task overwhelming. "Trying to enforce the law in Philadelphia," he remarked after giving up in disgust, "was worse than any battle I was ever in."[47]

Though corruption was widespread, it was not universal. There were many dedicated police officers, federal agents, and politicians who turned down bribes, despite the obvious temptation to accept them. But in an atmosphere of corruption and intimidation, they had difficulty prevailing. Faced with the realities of graft, many honest and competent rank-and-file agents chose to leave the force. And even when officials had not been corrupted, agents were often hamstrung by lack of money. Lawmakers seldom authorized funding increases to enforce the Volstead Act, and what extra funds they did supply were minimal. Like corruption, funding issues also drove capable agents into other careers. "I'm quitting," one assistant prosecutor told the press, "because too many little fellows with just hip quantities [small amounts of liquor] in their possession are caught, and the big chaps escape because the government hasn't got the facilities to catch them."[48]

Successful Agents

Still, the government did put time, effort, and money into a few well-publicized investigations of Volstead Act violations. Of all Prohibition agents, the best known was almost certainly a Chicago native named Eliot Ness. A philosophy major in college, Ness took a law enforcement job with the federal government because, as he put it, "it offered lots of

Daisy Simpson

A native of Northern California, Daisy Simpson was a petty criminal with what one journalist called "a weakness for narcotics" during the late 1910s. By 1920, however, Simpson had not only reformed but also had joined the San Francisco police force. When police chief Charles Goff was promoted to a new job enforcing the Volstead Act, he made Simpson one of the few female Prohibition agents.

Simpson was well suited for this work. She was dramatic, courageous, and very successful. Like other effective agents, Simpson was able to take on different personas as the situation demanded. "She could change her surface character like a chameleon," a newspaper article noted. "She entered into all her characters with a grace and perfection that would have aroused the envy of a finished actress. And to it all she brought a supreme daring and resourcefulness."

Stories of Simpson's ingenuity were many. Once she disguised herself as a helpless old woman and raided a speakeasy alone, taking five men prisoner at gunpoint. Often she pretended to be sick outside illegal bars, waiting for bartenders to come revive her with a sip of whiskey—whereupon she arrested them. During one three-week period, wrote a reporter, "she caused . . . the confiscation of 10,000 bottles of beer, 60 cases of gin, 12 cases of Scotch and a varied assortment of wines and liquors." But in 1926, a year after leaving the force, she returned to her roots. Arrested for drug use, she attempted suicide while awaiting trial and was eventually imprisoned.

Milwaukee (WI) Journal, "Stage Lost Great Actress in Daisy Simpson, Sleuth," July 4, 1926, pp. 6–7.

excitement."[49] He got what he wanted. By 1930 Ness was the leader of the Untouchables, a group of highly skilled agents charged with the task of bringing down Capone. Despite the dangers of taking on such a violent and powerful criminal, Ness and his team relished the assignment. The Untouchables never truly brought Capone to justice. Though the gangster was eventually jailed in the early 1930s, authorities convicted him only on charges of income tax evasion, rather than for bootlegging, extortion, and murder. Still, Ness's team did plenty to make Capone's life difficult, and their dogged investigation of Capone's activities helped lay the groundwork for his eventual conviction.

Ness was well known not merely because he was successful but also because he was dramatic. He would often tip off reporters and photographers in advance of a raid, guaranteeing that his activities would make the newspapers. Ness's exploits, moreover, were often worth reading about. The Untouchables were renowned for raiding illegal breweries and speakeasies, often in ways reminiscent of medieval warfare. The agents traveled in a huge truck equipped with battering rams and ladders, allowing them to break down doors and climb over walls as needed. They also disguised themselves as small-time gangsters and attended mob meetings, the better to learn what the gangs were up to. These masquerades was not always successful. At one such meeting Ness realized he was in trouble when he heard a nearby man ask a companion, "Shall I put a knife into him?"[50] Still, Ness survived the experience and other tight spots as well, becoming a national hero in the process.

Many other agents were nearly as effective. Among the best were Isadore Einstein and Moe Smith, a two-man team known to newspaper readers simply as Izzy and Moe. Based in New York, Izzy and Moe made nearly five thousand arrests during Prohibition. Like Ness, the two took on fake identities to gain access to speakeasies and liquor plants. At various times they passed themselves off as fishermen, streetcar conductors, musicians, and delegates to a political convention. Costumes were not always necessary, however. Because both men had forgettable features, their best disguise was often no disguise at all. At most, they carried props to allay suspicion. In one notable case, Izzy gained access to several illegal bars in part because he was carrying a bucket of pickles. "A fat man with pickles!," he chortled afterward. "Who'd ever think a fat man with pickles was an agent?"[51]

Crime fighters like Ness and the team of Izzy and Moe represented the best of Prohibition agents. Their exploits boosted the sagging reputations of the police during the era, and the sheer number of arrests they made indicated the effectiveness of their approach. But they were exceptions. Too many Prohibition agents did not pursue bootleggers as diligently as did the Untouchables. Too many were taking bribes from smugglers. Too many were intimidated by mob leaders. But even if all Prohibition agents had been completely dedicated to their jobs, there were too few enforcers to make much of a dent against the power, resources, and savagery of the gangs. The profits to be made in bootlegging made it virtually impossible to destroy the organized crime rings that sprang up to take advantage of Prohibition.

Chapter 4

Toward Repeal

Through the 1920s the architects of Prohibition continued to insist that the amendment was working. They cited statistics, many of them based more on wishful thinking than on reality, which revealed dramatic drops in drinking—90 percent or more since Prohibition had gone into effect. They pointed to places, mostly in rural areas, where drinking had been more or less stamped out altogether. They also cited the booming economy—and indeed, the twenties were a time of general prosperity—as evidence that Prohibition was having the desired effect. "Almost any dry could tell you," writes Frederick Lewis Allen, summing up the Prohibitionists' argument, "that prohibition had reduced the deaths from alcoholism, emptied the jails, and diverted the workman's dollar to the purchase of automobiles, radios, and homes. . . . Cases of poverty as a result of drunkenness were only a fraction of what they used to be."[52]

But by 1926 or so, an increasing number of Americans were finding this perspective impossible to accept. The optimism of the drys notwithstanding, the reality seemed very different. Other, more reliable statistics suggested that alcohol consumption had never fallen off by a figure approaching 90 percent—and that drinking was actually increasing. Whole neighborhoods were being taken over by gangs and bootleggers. In many cities, speakeasies were flourishing almost in plain sight. Prohibition had led to political corruption, given rise to organized crime, and lessened respect for laws and morality in general. In their estimation, Prohibition was not simply ineffective; it was a disaster.

As the 1920s turned to the 1930s, the wets' criticisms became increasingly difficult to dismiss. The dry lobby found itself more and more on the defensive, trying to explain to an impatient audience just why Prohibition remained a positive good for society. Support for Prohibition began to wane as police forces, editorial writers, and ordinary citizens came to the conclusion that the law was not working. "The large part of the population is sick of Prohibition that can't prohibit,"[53] wrote *The New York Times* in 1927. Before long, debate over the law moved back into the political sphere. But this time it was the wets who had momentum and organization and the drys who struggled to bring others to their viewpoint. By 1933 Prohibition, brought in to such acclaim and enthusiasm just thirteen years before, was on its way out.

A Losing Battle

This shift in public opinion did not by any means take place overnight. Rather, it was a gradual process, driven by a variety of events over a period of many years. The rise in organized crime was one of the most obvious factors. At first many Americans saw gangs as relatively harmless. As long as mob violence stayed well away from their daily lives, ordinary citizens were intrigued and often entertained by the gunfights, the turf battles, and other gangland occurrences. Some of the biggest gangs, moreover, offered assistance to struggling citizens in their territory. Capone, for example, provided housing and food to the poor in Chicago and in Lansing, Michigan, where he owned property. As one biographer describes it, to the people of Lansing "he was a friend, a benefactor, and in some cases a savior."[54] A few Thanksgiving dinners and occasional gifts of rent money bought Capone a lot of goodwill.

However, as time went on perspectives began to change. Public tolerance of gangland murders declined dramatically during the late 1920s, when the violence began spilling over to affect innocent people. City dwellers were often alarmed to see gangsters with shotguns patrolling their neighborhoods. That was especially true when shots aimed at other gunmen went astray, hitting and killing bystanders with no connection to any mob. In 1931, for example, New Yorkers were appalled when gangster Vincent Coll killed a five-year-old in a failed assassination attempt on another crime boss. It soon became clear, too, that those who spoke out against mobsters were taking a big risk. In

1930 Detroit radio broadcaster Gerald Buckley was killed, most likely by mob members, after devoting several of his programs to the problem of gang violence. In the wake of events like these, many who had supported Prohibition began to reconsider. As long as Prohibition continued, organized crime seemed unlikely to go away—and would probably get worse.

For many urban residents, moreover, it became increasingly clear that Prohibition was a losing battle. By the late 1920s police in cities such as Chicago, Philadelphia, and San Francisco had more or less given up trying to enforce the Volstead Act. In Detroit it was impossible to avoid noticing the boats churning across the river from Canada,

A lively speakeasy, serving an array of alcoholic beverages, attracts a well-heeled clientele in New York's Greenwich Village in 1933. Speakeasies flourished in cities all across the country during Prohibition.

Blaming the Victims

Since alcohol is necessary for some manufacturing processes, the government exempted certain industries from Prohibition. To ensure that this alcohol would not be used for drinking, however, the government mandated that industrial alcohol be denatured—that is, modified by adding a toxic substance called methanol. Methanol gives alcohol a terrible taste, and its consumption can cause blindness, even death. The addition of methanol was not especially effective, however. Some people were so desperate for a drink that they gulped down even denatured alcohol. Others were too drunk to tell the difference. Bootleggers, then, sometimes stole industrial alcohol and sold it to customers.

The consequences were predictable. During Prohibition, methanol blinded tens of thousands of Americans and killed thousands more. Many people blamed the government. In the late 1920s they called on officials to stop requiring denatured alcohol. But Wayne Wheeler, the Anti-Saloon League president, argued that those killed by the methanol had only themselves to blame. "People who drink bootleg beverages after the government has warned them of the danger," he proclaimed, "are in the same category as the man who goes into a drugstore, buys a bottle of carbolic acid with a label on it marked 'Poison,' and drinks the contents." Wheeler's words, however, repelled many ordinary Americans, who found them mean-spirited. His stand on this issue made Prohibitionists seem hard-hearted and unsympathetic, which contributed to the dwindling support for the Prohibition cause.

Quoted in Gerald Leinwand, *1927: High Tide of the 1920s*. New York: Four Walls Eight Windows, 2001, p. 83.

and the cars crossing the frozen waters during the winter. "There is general disregard for the law and scorn for it," wrote a sociologist about conditions in New Orleans. "Most of the men drink something every day."[55] From Baltimore to Boston, from St. Louis to Seattle, signs of illicit drinking were everywhere. Speakeasies, illegal distilleries, trucks transporting liquor right past police stations—it was sometimes hard to believe that Prohibition was actually in effect.

In most rural areas, the problems with enforcement were not nearly so obvious. Still, by the late 1920s it was evident to anyone who was paying attention that Prohibition was being widely ignored. If nothing else, the public statements of some government leaders confirmed it. In 1925, for example, an official admitted that at least 95 percent of all the alcohol being transported in the United States was evading the authorities. And an official report a few years later noted that demand for a product called corn sugar had risen dramatically since the beginning of Prohibition. In the words of the report's authors, corn sugar's legitimate uses were "few and not easy to ascertain"[56]—but it was a common ingredient in certain alcoholic drinks. The conclusion was clear: Corn sugar was adding to the nation's illegal alcohol supply. These and similar statistics further soured the public's mood on Prohibition.

The Judicial System

Another reason for the dwindling enthusiasm for Prohibition had to do with enforcement. The people of America had decidedly mixed feelings about enforcing the laws against alcohol. The result was that police captains and federal agents were criticized frequently, no matter what they did. In New York City, for instance, many observers charged that police were ignoring liquor violations. Government officials therefore adopted a new strategy, instructing officers to crack down on drinking and alcohol sales wherever they saw them. That shifted the force's focus radically—and, in the opinion of many other New Yorkers, foolishly. As some commentators pointed out, the police were now spending so much time dealing with liquor that they had time for little else. "It is demoralizing for the police force," said a judge. "Men are being stationed in restaurants to see [that] no one steals a drink, while around the corner a hold-up man is breaking into a jewelry shop."[57]

The judicial system's response to bootlegging and other violations of the liquor law was controversial too. One problem was the sheer number of cases brought to court. Prohibition agents—the honest ones, at least—were encouraged to pile up as many arrests as possible. Some of the arrests were for major violations of the law, such as hijacking shipments of industrial alcohol. Most, however, were for much less serious violations, such as selling a single bottle of beer. As a result, the courts were flooded with one minor alcohol-related case after another. Judicial districts across the country began spending half their time and energy on cases that involved the Volstead Act. Some were even more overwhelmed than that. One federal court in Alabama estimated that at one point, nine of every ten cases it heard dealt with Volstead violations.

To make matters even worse, the Volstead Act guaranteed a jury trial for anyone arrested for breaking the Prohibition laws. While this provision was a laudable attempt to preserve the civil rights of the accused, defendants quickly realized that they could turn it to their advantage. One reason was that juries were often sympathetic to those involved in the illegal liquor trade. Many jurors, especially in urban areas, enjoyed bootleg whiskey themselves and were unwilling to send someone to jail for alcohol-related offenses. "Juries will not convict if the punishment does not fit the crime,"[58] sighed Mabel Willebrandt, an official in charge of hiring and training Prohibition agents. She was right. Again and again jurors who sided with the wets acquitted the accused, ignoring even blatant evidence of Volstead Act violations.

The right to a jury gave defendants another advantage too. By demanding a jury instead of having their cases heard by a judge, they could slow the judicial process to the point where it could scarcely function. "There are many criminal cases pending . . . in Chicago for liquor violations," wrote one observer in 1922. "By a practically concerted action on the part of the defendants, they have all asked for a jury trial. If these cases were all tried before juries . . . the indictments which were returned last week by the grand jury would probably come to trial in 1924 or 1925."[59] Given this backlog, the courts had virtually no ability to deal with any other types of crimes.

Bargain Days and Injustice

There were several possible ways to solve this problem. The most obvious—hiring more judges and prosecutors—was also the most expensive, and government officials never seriously considered this approach. Instead, they chose to streamline the process. One plan of attack was to institute what officials referred to as bargain days. From time to time authorities would allow defendants to plead guilty to liquor-related crimes—with the guarantee that while they might have to pay fines, they would receive no jail time. "As a device to reduce a backlog of cases," writes legal historian Kenneth M. Murchison, "the bargain day was efficient. As a means of fairly enforcing [the law], it was suspect, to put the case mildly."[60]

Indeed, the system made no one happy. Drys were outraged that the bargain days existed at all. As they saw it, jail time was necessary to serve as a deterrent to those who were violating the law. For that matter, the drys noted, the fines did not do much to deter lawbreakers either; most of the fines were so small, often less than one hundred dollars, that bootleggers considered them to be a minor cost of doing business. "To call such fines 'convictions' is grotesque,"[61] declared a prominent prosecutor. But wets were discouraged too. To them, the overloaded court system was a clear indication that enforcing Prohibition was using up time and resources that would be better used to fight more serious crimes.

Nor did it help that when courts doled out justice at all, they doled it out unequally. Those who were convicted and sent to prison were disproportionately small-time offenders. Thanks to bribes and threats, members of large bootlegging gangs rarely faced prison time, no matter how serious the charges. Often, their cases never even came to trial, with charges being mysteriously dropped not long after arrest. Mobsters whose charges did not disappear relied on the assistance of fixers who

Protesters call for the repeal of Prohibition and the Volstead Act during a Fourth of July parade in New York City. By the late 1920s, groups began organizing for the purpose of changing or repealing the increasingly unpopular law.

spent their days in courthouses, offering jurors cash in exchange for a favorable verdict. Even when crimes moved from mere bootlegging to robbery, assault, and murder—as they often did—convictions were rare. During one stretch of the 1920s Chicago saw several hundred gang-related killings. Only one person, a low-level functionary in one of the city's mobs, received any jail time in connection with these deaths.

Organizations for Repeal

The problems with Prohibition became increasingly obvious as time progressed, By the mid-1920s, gangs were not only running rampant through the streets of major cities, but the judicial system seemed neither willing nor able to do its job. Corruption was spreading through virtually every level of government, and speakeasies and illegal distilleries continued to flourish. All of these factors helped shift public sentiment against Prohibition during the late 1920s. Organizations began springing up to urge changes in the law—or to push for abolishing Prohibition altogether. The Women's Committee for Repeal of the Eighteenth Amendment, for example, began working for abolition in 1927. Lawyers' groups in many states expressed their opposition to the amendment. So did influential business leaders and academics. "The Eighteenth Amendment represents the worst possible way of attempting to deal with the liquor traffic and the saloon,"[62] said Columbia University president Nicholas Murray Butler in 1927, and an increasing number of Americans were in agreement.

In 1928 the Democratic Party nominated New York governor Al Smith, an opponent of Prohibition, as their presidential candidate. Though Smith did not make repeal of Prohibition a major issue in his campaign, he made his distaste for the amendment clear. Smith lost the presidential race to Republican Herbert Hoover, a staunch dry, who lauded Prohibition as "a great social and economic experiment, noble in motive and far-reaching in purpose."[63] At the time, political pundits—especially those who thought the law was working well—interpreted Hoover's victory as a decisive win for Prohibition. In retrospect, however, the election was probably much less about Prohibition than it was about the economy. The country had been run by Republican presidents throughout the prosperous 1920s. While a vote for Hoover was in some sense a vote for Prohibition, it was more importantly a vote for a continuation of Republican economic policies.

Despite Smith's defeat at the polls, opponents of Prohibition continued to work for repeal of the amendment. The odds, however, were against them. A constitutional amendment cannot be overturned by a simple act of Congress or the passage of another ordinary law. It can only be replaced by another amendment, which would require opponents to convince a two-thirds majority in both houses of Congress to vote their way—and then, once again, get representatives from thirty-six states to agree. Even the most enthusiastic opponents of Prohibition were realistic about the difficulties they faced. And the drys, convinced that any attempt at rolling back Prohibition was doomed to failure, refused to take repeal attempts seriously. "There is as much chance of repealing the Eighteenth Amendment as there is for a hummingbird to fly to the planet Mars with the Washington Monument tied to its tail,"[64] remarked one ardent Prohibitionist.

The Great Depression

In late 1929, however, conditions changed abruptly. That October the US stock market crashed, wiping away any traces of an economic boom and plunging the country into the Great Depression. Over the next months the economy ground to a halt. Banks failed, stores closed, factories shuttered their doors. Millions of people were thrown out of work, with most who remained on the job taking substantial pay cuts. Government tax revenues slipped dramatically. Faced with a crisis of these proportions, many Americans argued that enforcement of Prohibition was both silly and wasteful. It seemed pointless to devote scarce federal funds to enforcement of the Volstead Act when so many people were going hungry. Moreover, properly regulated and taxed, liquor could become an important source of revenue for cash-strapped governments. Repeal, some claimed, could bring in $500 million in federal taxes alone. When Hoover dismissed these arguments, the wets formed new alliances to advocate for repeal. Drys did their best to discredit these groups—a newspaper dismissed one as a "drunken and immoral bunch of women"[65]—but the groups favoring repeal nonetheless got their message across.

By the early 1930s thousands of former supporters of Prohibition had joined the wet side. Hospital directors, social workers, judges, and others were admitting that despite the great promise of the new laws, Prohibition had proved completely ineffective. "It has not worked and never can work,"[66] conceded a prison official who had once been an ardent backer of the amendment. Business leader John D. Rockefeller, who had contributed hundreds of thousands of dollars to the dry cause,

The Sacramental Wine Racket

O ne of the bigger loopholes in the Volstead Act involved sacramental wine, which is used for religious purposes. Because wine is important in the rituals of some Christians and Jews, priests and rabbis could obtain limited amounts of wine for their congregations. Criminals quickly figured out ways to exploit the exemption, however, including getting laypeople to pass themselves off as ministers and rabbis. Because authorities did not check credentials carefully, hundreds of thousands of gallons of sacramental wine were sold to people who had no religious affiliation, let alone congregational responsibilities. Partly as a result, sales of sacramental wine soared during Prohibition.

A few legitimate priests and rabbis were involved in exploiting the loophole too. They saw an opportunity to earn extra money by selling sacramental wine. One Prohibition agent recalled a rabbi in Oakland, California, who distributed sacramental wine to people who were technically part of his congregation but in truth were no such thing. "This fellow had on the list of his congregation a lot of Irishmen," the agent remembered. "You'd have Mahoney and Flynn and many others who were not Jews or members of a legitimate congregation. [They would] come out with a gallon of port wine from the rabbi's house. Or a gallon of sherry—anything the rabbi blessed was good enough for sacramental purposes. Even a bottle of champagne!"

Quoted in Richard Mendelson, *From Demon to Darling: A Legal History of Wine in America.* Berkeley: University of California Press, 2009, p. 66.

renounced his support in 1932. Opposition to Prohibition was growing even among two groups no one had believed would ever waver in their support: Protestant ministers and the government administrators in charge of Prohibition enforcement.

Joyous crowds celebrate the end of Prohibition, as depicted in this illustration by a twentieth-century Italian artist. On December 5, 1933, Utah became the thirty-sixth state to approve the Twenty-First Amendment, thereby eliminating Prohibition.

By 1932 the Democrats had become closely identified with the forces calling for repeal. Indeed, delegates at the Democratic convention that year overwhelmingly approved a statement favoring repeal of Prohibition. "From this day on," their presidential candidate, Franklin D. Roosevelt, thundered in a speech to delegates, "the Eighteenth Amendment is doomed!"[67] Roosevelt swept to victory that November, handily defeating Hoover. Even before he took office in March 1933, his allies had already introduced a proposed Twenty-First Amendment in Congress. The language of this bill was extremely simple: "The eighteenth article of amendment to the Constitution of the United States," read the first section, "is hereby repealed."[68]

The Twenty-First Amendment

The drys did their best to block passage of the new amendment, but to no avail. Following what one newspaper referred to as a "brief but fervid debate that roused the packed galleries,"[69] the measure passed easily through both houses of Congress. Of the senators and representatives still in office who had voted in favor of the Eighteenth Amendment back in 1918, most now supported the new proposal. The bill then went to the states for ratification, which was not long in coming. Early in April, Michigan became the first state to ratify the Twenty-First amendment. By the end of June nine states had ratified. By the end of August the count stood at twenty. On December 5, 1933, Utah became the thirty-sixth state to approve the new amendment, putting the Twenty-First Amendment into the Constitution and eliminating the Eighteenth forever.

Some observers responded to the news with delight. "Free, free, free!!!!," wrote a federal judge after the new amendment had officially passed. "Curst be [Prohibition's] name, its memory, its parent, its fosterers, its designers, its sycophants, its proposers, its backers, its executors."[70] In New York City, Chicago, and Detroit, groups of revelers held parties and dances to display their delight at Prohibition's passing. Few Americans, it seemed, mourned Prohibition's loss. "There were not many friends of the 'deceased' at the funeral services,"[71] a Utah newspaper commented wryly, referring to the state convention at which delegates voted overwhelmingly to change the law.

Less than two decades earlier the Eighteenth Amendment had sailed through Congress, and state legislatures had vied with one another to ratify it as soon as possible. The millions of people who had supported the amendment were sure they were doing the right thing, sure that they were taking steps to make America a better, healthier, more moral place. Now the tide had shifted dramatically. Though no hummingbirds had flown to Mars, with or without the Washington Monument in tow, Prohibition was over. In the end, it had fallen apart from the weight of its own failures. By sparking the rise of organized crime, by paralyzing the judicial system, by encouraging corruption, and by turning occasional and moderate drinkers into criminals, the law had proved unworkable, unenforceable, and unfair. It was no wonder, then, that Americans finally chose to drop it altogether.

Chapter 5

What Is the Legacy of Prohibition?

After the Eighteenth Amendment was repealed, American alcohol use returned to what it had been in the days before the Volstead Act. Liquor stores and bars reopened, and breweries that had been converted into cereal plants or ice cream factories returned to the beer business. For Americans who had continued drinking throughout Prohibition, drinking was again something that could be done entirely in the open. And those who had obeyed the Volstead Act, whether from fear of being arrested or from a belief that laws should always be followed, could now drink as they had before 1920.

But although alcohol use had regained its former legal status, the world had become a very different place. Repeal could not return American society to what it had been before 1920. The intervening years had brought new inventions, new ideas, and other changes that had little to do with Prohibition. These included the growth of radio, the proliferation of cars, and the rapid expansion of cities. Still, the world had also changed in ways that were directly due to Prohibition. What Hoover had referred to as the "great social and economic experiment"[72] had significantly altered American society in ways that continue to resonate today.

The End of Bootlegging

In the wake of Prohibition's repeal, no change was as obvious as the effect on bootlegging. Smugglers, speakeasy owners, and illegal distillers had made millions from alcohol during the Prohibition era precisely because liquor was illegal. With no legal competition, they had been able to charge whatever they wanted for their product. With the legalization of liquor, however, bootleggers' circumstances changed dramatically. Legitimate liquor stores and bars had no need to charge high prices. In most places, the bottom dropped out of the illegal liquor market. Rumrunning no longer paid. Repeal had ended the career of the average bootlegger.

The end of bootlegging had a huge effect on parts of the United States. In Detroit, where bootlegging ranked behind only car manufacturing among the city's major industries, stopping the flow of illegal beer, wine, and whiskey caused economic distress. While a few bootleggers sought to make a living as legitimate liquor sellers and distributors, most did not; they knew they could not match their bootlegging earnings as legitimate businessmen. The same was true in other cities. Social reformer Jane Addams had once expressed her belief that "all bootleggers would oppose a change in the [Prohibition] law,"[73] and to judge from the loss of income that many bootleggers experienced after repeal, she was probably correct.

If the change caused by the end of bootlegging was significant in the United States, the situation was worse in foreign regions where the economy relied heavily on the manufacture of liquor bound for the United States. The tiny French islands known as Saint-Pierre and Miquelon represented an excellent example. Throughout the 1920s and early 1930s these islands, located off the coast of Newfoundland, Canada, had been major providers of liquor for the northeastern United States. As bootleg liquor had flowed out of the islands, money had flowed in, making some people very wealthy. Now, the glory days were over. "The end of Prohibition in 1933," reports a news organization, "plunged the islands into economic depression."[74]

Organized Crime Continues

Though bootlegging largely disappeared after 1933, the same cannot be said of organized crime. The mobs that dominated bootlegging during Prohibition had already branched out into other criminal endeavors by the end of the 1920s. Though in 1927 Capone was making an esti-

Bootlegging During the 1950s and 1960s

The end of Prohibition did not mean the end of bootlegging altogether. Rumrunning remained a sometimes-thriving business in a few areas of the country where Prohibition-style laws still barred the sale and manufacture of alcohol within state, county, or city borders. In Mississippi, for example, where liquor remained illegal until the 1960s, enterprising bootleggers continued to earn money smuggling alcohol into the state for many years after the death of national Prohibition. That bootlegging remained lucrative for Mississippians was clear from a comment made by one rumrunner when the state put its ban on alcohol up for a public vote. "For the sake of my family," he urged his neighbors, "vote dry!"

Still, in comparison with the number of people affected by the Volstead Act, the population affected by local and state prohibitions after 1933 was trivial. In 1960, for instance, Mississippi had just over 2 million people—about as many as the city of Philadelphia, Pennsylvania, at that time. The market for illegal alcohol during the 1950s and 1960s, then, was quite small. Whatever a Mississippi bootlegger of the 1950s could earn was a far cry from what the urban bootleggers of the twenties had made. As a result, bootlegging in the years following Prohibition's repeal was largely the work of small operators. Without an opportunity to earn the enormous profits of the Prohibition era, big gangs had little interest in rumrunning after 1933.

Quoted in Daniel Okrent, *Last Call.* New York: Scribner, 2010, p. 375.

mated $60 million a year from the production and sale of alcohol, for example, his business empire as a whole was worth much more. Capone's investments in illegal gambling halls, brothels, and the like were bringing in millions more each year by that time.

Other gangsters followed Capone's lead. Unwilling to give up on the enormous profits they had raked in through bootlegging, most mobsters chose not to go legitimate when Prohibition ended. Like Capone, they had become involved in other illegal activities by the middle to late 1920s. Once Prohibition ended, they threw themselves into these businesses with even more enthusiasm. In Newport, Kentucky, for example, the end of Prohibition saw not only a rise in the number of prostitutes but also an increase in the number of brothels that were run by organized crime syndicates. In Cleveland, similarly, illegal casinos began multiplying soon after the passage of the Twenty-First Amendment.

Many of the former rumrunners also became racketeers. These men, usually affiliated with organized crime rings, would offer storekeepers and manufacturers a deal. In exchange for a sizeable cash payment, the gangsters would promise to protect the business from damage. In theory, at least, the business owner was free to accept the offer or to reject it. In practice, however, there was no choice. As Allen writes, "The victim soon learned that if he did not pay, his shop would be bombed, or his trucks wrecked, or he himself might be shot in cold blood." And as in Prohibition, law enforcement officials could not be relied upon to help; in Allen's words, "the authorities were frightened or fixed [bribed]."[75]

Prohibition's Criminal Legacy

With gambling, racketeering, and other activities, the organized crime rings of the later 1930s and the 1940s were often making nearly as much money as their counterparts of the Prohibition era. They were also causing nearly as much mayhem. In 1934, for example, New York gangster Vito Genovese arranged the murder of rival mobster Ferdinand Boccia. The following year another New York gang leader, Dutch Schultz, was gunned down by men in the employ of racketeer Lucky Luciano. And just as violence continued at the same level as during Prohibition, so too did organized crime's influence on government. In 1951, when the US Senate held a series of hearings on the problem of crime rings, participants concluded that organized crime was so widespread that it threatened the foundations of American freedom and democracy as well. Not much, as it turned out, had changed since Prohibition.

Even today, organized crime rings remain powerful. "They bring drugs into our cities," reports the FBI, "and raise the level of violence in our communities by buying off corrupt officials and using graft, extortion, intimidation, and murder to maintain their operations."[76] Though law enforcement has done a great deal to limit racketeering and gang involvement in gambling, the organized gangs of the 2000s still participate in these activities. They have also developed other ways to make money, including a few (such as Internet fraud, identity theft,

California brewery workers celebrate the end of Prohibition. With the repeal of the Eighteenth Amendment, breweries that had been converted to other purposes returned to the beer-making business, liquor stores reopened, and Americans once again drank alcohol without fear of prosecution.

and the illegal copying and distribution of CDs and DVDs) that would be unfamiliar to the gangs of the 1920s.

In other ways, though, modern crime rings are very similar to their predecessors of the 1920s. In particular, the typical crime ring of the modern era earns much of its money from the manufacture and sale of illegal substances, notably drugs such as cocaine and heroin. Just as the mobsters of the 1920s smuggled liquor across the US border, the mobsters of today import marijuana and other drugs from abroad. Just as gang members of 1926 or 1932 set up illegal distilleries and brewing companies, gang members of today produce cocaine or methamphetamines in isolated labs and converted warehouses. Though Al Capone and the Purples are no more, they would instantly recognize this aspect of modern mob business.

Prohibition did not *create* America's organized crime problem. Crime flourished in the United States from its earliest days, and crime rings were certainly active before Prohibition became law. Moreover, other social and technological changes affected the rise of organized crime during the 1920s. These included, for instance, the increasing use of the automobile, which made it easy for robbers and hit men to flee from crime scenes. It also included the development of new and increasingly deadly firearms, without which the gang violence of the 1920s would have been considerably less bloody. And the unrestrained growth of cities brought places like New York, Detroit, and Chicago to a point where policing them became extremely difficult.

Still, Prohibition did have an impact on organized crime in America. The ban on alcohol, more than any other factor, was responsible for making organized crime the force it was through much of the later twentieth century—and to a degree, what it remains even today. The ban on alcohol, along with the tremendous profits that could be made from violating it, spurred an unprecedented rise in gang violence, gang-related corruption, and, perhaps most important, gang power. As Allen concludes,

> Fill a man's pockets with money, give him a chance at a huge profit, put him into an illegal business and thus deny him recourse to the law if he is attacked, and you have made it easy for

him to bribe and shoot. . . . It is ironically true . . . that the out-
burst of corruption and crime . . . in the nineteen-twenties was
immediately occasioned by the attempt to banish the tempta-
tions of liquor from the American home.[77]

Tourism and Las Vegas

In addition to the growth of organized crime, Prohibition has had
other long-lasting effects—most of them not nearly as violent. The
tourist industry in the Bahamas, for example, was sparked in part by
the collapse of the bootleg liquor industry in the Caribbean. Eager
to continue the regular influx of money into their islands, Bahamian
officials cast around for something new to replace the funds once
earned from rumrunning. They hit on tourism as a possible solution. As one local leader argued, "If we can't take the liquor to the
Americans, we must bring the Americans to the liquor."[78] Given the
islands' warm climate and short distance from the United States, this
was a wise decision; the Bahamas remain a desirable destination for
US tourists today.

Las Vegas, Nevada, is yet another legacy of Prohibition. During the 1930s, unlike other states, Nevada permitted casino gambling statewide and had legal prostitution in many counties. This
permissive ethos made Nevada attractive to organized crime figures
following Prohibition's repeal. Some moved to Las Vegas, turning the
once-sleepy town into a high-powered destination for tourists, businesses, and conventions. Within a few years of Prohibition's demise,
the change was well under way as developers began building larger
and larger casinos, complete with hotels, theaters, and other entertainment venues. "From the 1940s through the 1970s," a history of
the city notes, "Las Vegas and its lavish resorts were made possible in
large part by the mob, who not only funded resort development, but
offered indispensable knowledge in casino management."[79] Today, in
large part because of Prohibition's repeal, Las Vegas ranks among the
world's most popular vacation spots.

Prohibition, Morality, and Politics

A final important legacy of Prohibition has to do with political discourse. Part of the debate over Prohibition revolved around the question of government's role in American society. The Prohibitionists believed that government should be used as a tool to get people to behave in moral and decent ways. If Americans could not police themselves where alcohol was concerned—and as the Prohibitionists saw it in the early 1900s, they certainly could not—then it was incumbent on the government to save people from themselves by banning the substance that caused the problems. Those unwilling to act to preserve morality, in the eyes of the Prohibitionists, were endangering not only themselves and their families but were also jeopardizing the future of the community and the country. "My boys may go to ruin through the legalized saloon by YOUR consent," read a pro–Eighteenth Amendment advertisement criticizing those who did not support Prohibition, "but *your* boys never will by *my* consent."[80]

The Prohibitionists argued that easy access to alcohol caused major problems for the drinker, and in many cases that was undeniable. For those who drank to excess, alcohol was a serious issue. Drunks spent much of their time passed out in the gutter, men and women died of alcohol-related diseases, and drunken people were unable to stay employed. Likewise, those who favored Prohibition often pointed out that alcohol was an overarching social problem, one that affected more than just the individual drinker, and to some degree that was true as well. When men of the late 1800s and early 1900s drank too much, for example, their families suffered too. The bar brawls associated with legal saloons, similarly, used precious police resources. The Prohibitionists' argument that banning alcohol could help protect and improve society was correct—in theory, if not in practice.

But for many, if not most, Prohibitionists, the objection they had to alcohol was not so much about the social costs of drinking; rather, it was about drinking itself. To the drys of the 1920s and earlier, alcohol was an objectionable substance by its very nature. Their rhetoric insisted that alcohol was poison, not just for the body but also for the soul. Indeed, many of the drys associated strong drink with the devil. Evan-

The Decline of Harlem

Located in northern Manhattan, Harlem was the center of black culture during the 1920s. African American writers such as Langston Hughes and Zora Neale Hurston lived and worked in Harlem; so did musicians such as Duke Ellington and Marian Anderson. Harlem was especially well known for its nightclubs, where patrons—many of them white—went to hear African Americans perform jazz, the blues, and other popular music.

At the time Harlem's nightclubs held another attraction besides music: the easy availability of alcohol. Most clubs offered their visitors a large selection of high-quality drinks. Police raids on the clubs were rare, moreover, so audiences in the nightclubs could drink in peace. Despite Harlem's distance from the wealthier, whiter parts of Manhattan, the combination of alcohol and music helped Harlem rank among the trendiest parts of town during the twenties.

By World War II, though, Harlem had entered a decline, and many of the nightclubs had closed. Part of the reason was the Great Depression, which limited the funds people had for entertainment. Part was the fickle nature of music aficionados, many of whom had moved on to other passions since the twenties. But the end of Prohibition played a role in Harlem's decline too. During its heyday, Harlem had often been considered *the* place to go to get a drink. Once drinks could be had anywhere, some of Harlem's glamour and appeal was lost. Repealing Prohibition thus helped bring the era of Harlem's cultural dominance to a close.

gelist Billy Sunday called alcoholic beverages "God's worst enemy"[81]; another activist described liquor as "the dark beverage of hell."[82] Given such animosity, it is not surprising that alcohol became a moral issue for many Americans. Since an upstanding, God-fearing person would never touch alcohol, drinking was only for the immoral: backsliders, degenerates, and worse. The goal of Prohibition, for many of its supporters, was to eliminate a great moral evil from the earth.

Legislating Morality

In some ways the argument over Prohibition continues today. Over and over again Americans have sought to outlaw certain products and behaviors, though not usually through a Constitutional amendment, and have fought to keep certain other products and behaviors from becoming legalized. Their reasons often focus on the perceived social costs of these activities and goods. But morality is frequently a part of the debate as well. Just as alcohol was perceived by many to be immoral in and of itself, those trying to prevent prostitution, drug use, and other activities and products today are often driven by concerns about their effects on the moral fabric of America. Supporters of these bans rarely if ever cite Prohibition as their model, but the connection is clear.

Opponents of government action in cases like these, in contrast, are quick to bring Prohibition into the discussion. To them the lesson of Prohibition is evident. As a famous saying goes, "You can't legislate morality."[83] In their eyes any attempt to eliminate a product or service on moral grounds is doomed to failure. People will simply find ways to get around the ban, and in the process of stamping it out, society will likely be affected for the worse. The same moral beliefs that drove the Prohibitionists, then, form part of the foundation of today's debates over any number of social problems. The arguments offered pro and con in these debates are familiar to anyone acquainted with the discussion over Prohibition.

Opponents of bans frequently cite the nation's experiences with Prohibition as a reason for their stance. This mindset prevails on both ends of the political spectrum. Arguing against laws designed to protect people's health by limiting access to fatty foods, for instance, conservative political commentator Anthony Gregory charges that these efforts represent an assault on Americans' civil liberties. To him, the goal of limiting Americans' individual choices is reminiscent of the excesses of Prohibition. Though to date no one has seriously suggested that the government outlaw the manufacture or sale of junk food and sugary drinks, Gregory sees this as a logical—and unacceptable—next step. "The puritanical mindset behind alcohol prohibition persists,"[84] he writes.

Other commentators make similar arguments from the left, again citing Prohibition as a model that should never again be followed. Prostitution is one example. By keeping prostitution illegal, some liberals argue, the United States is making essentially the same mistake it made with Prohibition. Certainly, just as was true with drinking during the era of Prohibition, the fact that prostitution is against the law does little to prevent it from happening. Most current estimates suggest that prostitution is a multibillion-dollar business in the United States. And again, as with alcohol sales during the Prohibition years, banning prostitution pushes it underground, where it is neither taxed nor regulated. "Let us reject antique moralism,"[85] writes one advocate of legalizing prostitution, attacking the Prohibition-based notion that government should uphold virtuous behavior.

The War on Drugs

The modern debate that most clearly tracks the Prohibition era, however, deals with illegal drugs such as cocaine, methamphetamines, and especially marijuana. With few exceptions, these drugs are illegal across the United States today. The penalties for possessing them, let alone selling or manufacturing them, can be extremely harsh. One reason that these substances are off-limits is health. For many of these drugs there is overwhelming evidence that they have negative effects on the body and the mind. However, there is also no question that part of the opposition to drug use is based on morality. As one anti-drug blogger puts it, "Illegal drug use is not the sort of activity in which a morally serious person will be involved."[86]

The result of these moral and practical concerns is the so-called war on drugs—a long-term battle to keep drugs out of the hands of

Americans. While many police officers, politicians, and ordinary citizens wholeheartedly support this fight against drug use, others are much less enthusiastic. Indeed, for many observers, the war on drugs has very little to recommend it. The fight, they point out, is extremely costly, with local, state, and federal governments spending a total of $30 billion to $40 billion each year on enforcement efforts. To these observers, moreover, the emphasis on drugs diverts law enforcement from attacking other, more serious crimes. "Someone is arrested for violating a drug law every 19 seconds,"[87] points out one advocacy group. Indeed, over half of all federal prisoners were originally sentenced on drug charges.

To these opponents, the war on drugs is uncomfortably reminiscent of the Prohibition era. As they see it, regardless of any moral concerns that may be connected with drug use, the war on drugs is no more ef-

In 2011 a Southern California woman expresses her views regarding prohibitions on marijuana. The lessons of Prohibition continue to resonate with those who debate efforts to control behavior through bans on marijuana and other drugs, sugary sodas, fatty foods, and more.

fective in removing drugs from society than Prohibition was in ending alcohol use. As with the prohibition of alcohol under the Volstead Act, criminalizing drug use, these opponents argue, simply drives drug use into the shadows. This policy allows gangs to supply drugs, makes it impossible for governments to obtain tax revenue on sales of these substances, and endangers drug users because they cannot come to the police over a dispute with a drug dealer.

Indeed, some people who support changes to drug laws draw explicit parallels between Prohibition's failures and the drug policies in today's United States. Colorado sheriff and author Bill Masters, for example, titled a recent book on the drug laws *The New Prohibition*. Though Masters began his law enforcement career as a staunch advocate of the war on drugs, he has since changed his mind, in part because he views the struggle to control drug use as a second—and equally ill-fated—example of Prohibition. Similarly, an organization dedicated to changing drug laws uses the slogan "Remember Prohibition? It Still Doesn't Work." [88] A poster issued by this group makes the connection unmistakable: It includes the slogan against a backdrop of Prohibition-era rumrunners wielding shotguns.

Those who support the drug laws as they currently stand, of course, dispute any connection between the government's drug policy and Prohibition. For the most part, they do not ignore the argument made by those who would like to change the drug laws. Instead, they point out the differences between the early twentieth-century attempt to prohibit alcohol and modern attempts to limit drugs. Comparisons, they argue, are invalid. "Prohibition was enforced on a substance that was deeply rooted in our culture," one commentator points out. "It may have been much more effective given another generation or two." Drugs, in contrast, never were legal, and never held such an important place in American society. "It's a bad comparison that proves nothing," the writer concludes, "because the circumstances were much different."[89]

Determining the balance between a government that is too active in protecting its citizens and a government that is not active enough has always been tricky. How government should respond to issues of drug use, prostitution, and even obesity will remain a heated topic of discussion for the foreseeable future. The argument, however, would not be what it is today without the example of Prohibition. The Prohibition era offers Americans on one side of these issues a model of what to try—and ideas of what to do differently to improve the outcome. Likewise, for Americans on the other side of the divide, Prohibition is an example of the unintended consequences of trying to legislate how people act. Without Prohibition as a touchstone, the debate would be very different.

Source Notes

Chapter One: What Conditions Led to Prohibition?

1. Mark Edward Lender, *Drinking in America: A History.* New York: Simon and Schuster, 1987, p. 5.
2. Lender, *Drinking in America*, p. 12.
3. Thomas Ford, *A History of Illinois, from Its Commencement as a State in 1818 to 1847.* Chicago: S.C. Griggs, 1854, p. 104.
4. Edward Wakin, *Enter the Irish-American.* New York: Thomas Y. Crowell, 1976, p. 59.
5. Michael Clifford, "Sobering Lessons for Young Irish Abroad," *Irish Examiner* (Lapps Quay, Cork, IE), June 30, 2012. www.irishexam iner.com.
6. Jacob Riis, *How the Other Half Lives.* New York: Scribner's, 1914, p. 4.
7. Nathan Bangs, *A History of the Methodist Episcopal Church.* New York: Carlton and Phillips, 1853, p. 96.
8. Quoted in Gerald Leinwand, *1927: High Tide of the Twenties.* New York: Four Walls Eight Windows, 2001, p. 78.
9. Quoted in Hasia R. Diner, *Erin's Daughters: Irish Immigrant Women in the Nineteeth Century.* Baltimore: Johns Hopkins University Press, 1983, p. 56.
10. Benjamin Rush, *An Inquiry into the Effects of Ardent Spirits upon the Human Body and Mind.* Boston: James Loring, 1823, p. 11.
11. Rush, *An Inquiry into the Effects of Ardent Spirits Upon the Human Body and Mind*, p. 17.
12. Quoted in David Brion Davis, *Antebellum American Culture: An Interpretive Anthology.* State College: Pennsylvania State University Press, 1979, p. 395.
13. Quoted in William R. Hutchison, *Religious Pluralism in America.* New Haven, CT: Yale University Press, 2004, p. 102.

14. Quoted in *American Experience,* "People & Events: Carrie Nation," Public Broadcasting System. www.pbs.org.

15. Quoted in Bangs, *A History of the Methodist Episcopal Church,* p. 93.

16. Quoted in John W. Frick, *Theatre, Culture, and Temperance Reform in Nineteenth-Century America.* Cambridge, UK: Cambridge University Press, 2003, p. 156.

17. Quoted in John Newton Stearns, ed., *Temperance in All Nations.* Vol. 2. New York: National Temperance Society, 1893, p. 328.

Chapter Two: Prohibition Begins

18. *Pella (IA) Chronicle,* "The Liquor Traffic," December 10, 1914, p. 7.

19. Ernest Cherrington, *History of the Anti-Saloon League.* Westerville, OH: American Issue, 1913, p. 83.

20. Cherrington, *History of the Anti-Saloon League,* p. 106.

21. Quoted in Michael Lerner, *Dry Manhattan.* Cambridge, MA: Harvard University Press, 2007, p. 10.

22. Quoted in Albert Shaw, ed., *The American Review of Reviews.* Vol. 58. New York: Review of Reviews, 1919, p. 79.

23. Quoted in Elizabeth Stevenson, *Babbitts and Bohemians.* New York: Macmillan, 1967, p. 89.

24. Quoted in National Archives, "The Constitution of the United States, Amendments 11–27." www.archives.gov.

25. Quoted in Richard Mendelson, *From Demon to Darling: A Legal History of Wine in America.* Berkeley: University of California Press, 2009, p. 68.

26. Frederick Lewis Allen, *Only Yesterday.* New York: Harper and Row, 1931, p. 249.

27. Daniel Okrent, *Last Call.* New York: Scribner, 2010, p. 112.

28. Allen, *Only Yesterday,* p. 250.

29. *Kokomo (IN) Tribune,* "Reign of Demon Rum Now Ended," January 17, 1920, p. 8.

30. Quoted in Leinwand, *1927,* p. 78.

31. Quoted in Okrent, *Last Call,* p. 2.

32. Quoted in Okrent, *Last Call*, p. 119.

33. Allen, *Only Yesterday*, p. 249.

34. *Ironwood (MI) Daily Globe,* "Reveals Profit in Bootlegging," November 3, 1921, p. 1.

35. *Steubenville (OH) Herald-Star,* "Nation Made Dry by States Voting for Prohibition," January 16, 1919, p. 1.

Chapter Three: Organized Crime and Law Enforcement

36. *Galveston (TX) Daily News,* "Bootleggers at Work," January 8, 1905, p. 8.

37. *Ironwood (MI) Daily Globe,* "Reveals Profit in Bootlegging," p. 1.

38. Quoted in Lerner, *Dry Manhattan*, p. 58.

39. *Ironwood (MI) Daily Globe,* "Reveals Profit in Bootlegging," p. 1.

40. Quoted in Okrent, *Last Call*, p. 252.

41. Stevenson, *Babbitts and Bohemians*, p. 92.

42. *Times Magazine,* "Mobsters, Mayhem & Murder," 2006. www .walkervilletimes.com.

43. Allen, *Only Yesterday*, pp. 260–61.

44. *Wisconsin Rapids Daily Tribune,* "Local Man Sees Massacre Victims," February 15, 1929, p. 1.

45. Lerner, *Dry Manhattan*, p. 74.

46. Quoted in Stevenson, *Babbitts and Bohemians*, p. 89.

47. Quoted in Okrent, *Last Call*, p. 204.

48. Quoted in *Ironwood (MI) Daily Globe*, "Congress Urged to Start Probe," November 4, 1921, p. 6.

49. Quoted in *New Castle (PA) News*, "Hunt Underworld for Members of Capone's Gang," June 13, 1931, p. 5.

50. Quoted in *New Castle (PA) News*, "Hunt Underworld for Members of Capone's Gang," p. 5.

51. Quoted in Isabel Leighton, ed., *The Aspirin Age, 1919–1941.* New York: Simon and Schuster, 1949, p. 41.

Chapter Four: Toward Repeal

52. Allen, *Only Yesterday*, pp. 254–55.

53. Quoted in Leinwand, *1927*, p. 84.

54. Laurence Bergreen, *Capone: The Man and the Era*. New York: Simon and Schuster, 1994, p. 177.

55. Quoted in Okrent, *Last Call*, p. 258.

56. Quoted in Allen, *Only Yesterday*, p. 253.

57. Quoted in Lerner, *Dry Manhattan*, p. 78.

58. Quoted in Okrent, *Last Call*, p. 253.

59. Quoted in Kenneth M. Murchison, *Federal Criminal Law Doctrines: The Forgotten Influence of National Prohibition*. Durham, NC: Duke University Press, 1994, pp. 159–60.

60. Murchison, *Federal Criminal Law Doctrines*, p. 160.

61. Quoted in Okrent, *Last Call*, p. 254.

62. Quoted in Leinwand, *1927*, p. 80.

63. Quoted in Allen, *Only Yesterday*, p. 256.

64. Quoted in Okrent, *Last Call*, p. 330.

65. Quoted in Lerner, *Dry Manhattan*, p. 278.

66. Quoted in Lerner, *Dry Manhattan*, p. 285.

67. Quoted in *American Heritage*, "1933: Fifty Years Ago," December 1983. www.americanheritage.com.

68. Quoted in Okrent, *Last Call*, pp. 351–52.

69. *Portsmouth (OH) Times*, "House Votes to Submit Dry Repeal," February 20, 1933, p. 1.

70. Quoted in Lerner, *Dry Manhattan*, p. 306.

71. *Salt Lake Tribune*, "Utah Vote Ends Prohibition Era," December 6, 1933, p. 1.

Chapter Five: What Is the Legacy of Prohibition?

72. Quoted in Allen, *Only Yesterday*, p. 256.

73. Quoted in Okrent, *Last Call*, p. 302.

74. BBC News, "Regions and Territories: St. Pierre and Miquelon," November 2, 2011. http://news.bbc.co.uk.

75. Allen, *Only Yesterday*, p. 267.

76. Federal Bureau of Investigation, "Organized Crime: Overview." www.fbi.gov.

77. Allen, *Only Yesterday*, p. 264.

78. Quoted in Michael Craton and Gail Saunders, *Islanders in the Stream: A History of the Bahamian People.* Vol. 2. Athens: University of Georgia Press, 1998, p. 264.

79. Quoted in PBS, "American Experience: Las Vegas, an Unconventional History." http://www.pbs.org.

80. Quoted in *Lewiston (ME) Daily Sun,* "Little Shines," November 5, 1904, p. 4.

81. Quoted in Okrent, *Last Call,* p. 97.

82. Quoted in S.S. Hamill, *The Science of Elocution.* New York: Phillips and Hunt, 1886, p. 312.

83. Quoted in D. Brad Wright, "Legislating Morality," *Huffington Post,* September 9, 2009. www.huffingtonpost.com.

84. Anthony Gregory, "Enduring Legacy of Prohibition," Independent Institute, December 3, 2009. www.independent.org.

85. Carol Leigh, "Labor Laws, Not Criminal Laws, Are the Solution," *New York Times,* April 19, 2012. www.nytimes.com.

86. Jim Spiegel, "Why Illegal Drug Use Is Immoral," *Wisdom & Folly* (blog), April 21, 2010. http://wisdomandfollyblog.com.

87. Drug Sense, "Drug War Clock." www.drugsense.org.

88. Quoted in Broward Law Blog, "I Am Patient Number 380206011," March 9, 2009. http://browardlawblog.blogspot.com.

89. Quoted in Gamefaqs, "Politics," March 1, 2012. www.gamefaqs .com.

Important People of Prohibition

Al Capone: Chicago-based bootlegger and organized crime figure who earned hundreds of millions of dollars during Prohibition.

Ernest Cherrington: Temperance journalist and a leader in the Anti-Saloon League.

Herbert Hoover: President toward the end of Prohibition and supporter of the Eighteenth Amendment.

Carry Nation: Ardent temperance worker who destroyed saloons using a hatchet.

Eliot Ness: Prohibition agent and leader of the Untouchables, a group of highly skilled agents charged with the task of bringing down gangster Al Capone.

Franklin D. Roosevelt: President of the United States at the end of Prohibition; an opponent of the Eighteenth Amendment.

Benjamin Rush: A doctor and politician who was an early voice in support of temperance.

Al Smith: Democratic Party presidential candidate in 1928 and a noted opponent of Prohibition.

Andrew J. Volstead: US Representative from Minnesota for whom the Volstead Act was named.

Frances E. Willard: Founder of the anti-alcohol Women's Christian Temperance Union.

Woodrow Wilson: President of the United States when Prohibition was made law.

For Further Research

Books

Edward Behr, *Prohibition: Thirteen Years That Changed America*. New York: Arcade, 2011.

Karen Blumenthal, *Bootleg: Murder, Moonshine, and the Lawless Years of Prohibition*. New York: Roaring Brook, 2011.

John M. Dunn, *Prohibition*. Detroit: Lucent, 2010.

Charles Henry Gervais, *The Rumrunners: A Prohibition Scrapbook*. Emeryville, Ontario, CAN: Biblioasis, 2009.

Michael Lerner, *Dry Manhattan: Prohibition in New York City*. Cambridge, MA: Harvard University Press, 2007.

Daniel Okrent, *Last Call: The Rise and Fall of Prohibition, 1920–1933*. New York: Scribner, 2010.

Websites

National Public Radio, "Prohibition Life: Politics, Loopholes, and Bathtub Gin" (www.npr.org/2010/05/10/126613316/prohibition-life -politics-loopholes-and-bathtub-gin). This web page is an audio of a broadcast interview with Daniel Okrent, author of a book about Prohibition; the page also includes an excerpt from the book and some background information.

New York Times, "Joe Sent Me" (www.nytimes.com/slideshow/2009 /06/02/dining/20090603-speakeasy-slideshow_index.html?ref=prohib itionera19201933). This web page presents a series of images from the Prohibition era.

Ohio State University History Department, "Temperance and Prohibition" (http://prohibition.osu.edu). This site contains links to articles about Prohibition, primary source materials, and other materials related to the era.

Prohibition Party (www.prohibitionparty.org). The Prohibition Party is a small American political organization; its goals regarding alcohol include a return to Prohibition and a stronger version of the Volstead Act. The site includes information about the party's platform and activities.

Public Broadcasting System, *Prohibition* (www.pbs.org/kenburns /prohibition). This is a companion site to the Ken Burns documentary *Prohibition.* It includes background information on the people and events of the period.

Index

Note: Boldface page numbers indicate illustrations.

Picture Credits

Cover: F&A Archive/The Art Archive at Art Resource, NY

© Bettmann/Corbis: 10, 58, 69

© Stefano Bianchetti/Corbis: 14

Bpk, Berlin/Art Resource, NY: 62

Culver Pictures/The Art Archive at Art Resource, NY: 35

Museum of the City of New York/The Art Archive at Art Resource, NY: 53

© Kevin Sullivan/Zuma Press/Corbis: 76

Thinkstock Images: 6, 7

© Underwood & Underwood/Corbis: 29

Maury Aaseng: 23

Carry Nation, the Kansas Saloon smasher (sepia photo), American Photographer, (20th century)/Private Collection/The Stapleton Collection/The Bridgeman Art Library: 21

Bootleggers during Prohibition (b/w photo), American Photographer, (20th century)/Historical Museum of Southern Florida, Miami, USA/© HistoryMiami/The Bridgeman Art Library: 41

The Birger Gang, of Southern Illinois, 1924 (b/w photo), American Photographer, (20th century)/Private Collection/Peter Newark American Pictures/The Bridgeman Art Library: 45

About the Author

Stephen Currie has written dozens of books, including *Goblins, The Black Death,* and *Hydropower* for ReferencePoint Press. He has also published educational materials, newspaper articles, and short stories, and he has taught at various grade levels ranging from kindergarten through college. He lives in Dutchess County, New York.